Milwaukee & N R Co v. Brooks Locomotive Works U.S. Supreme Court Transcript of Record with Supporting Pleadings

U.S. Supreme Court, E MARINER, Additional Contributors

Milwaukee & N R Co v. Brooks Locomotive Works
Transcript of Record / U.S. Supreme Court / 1886 / 226 / 121 U.S. 430 / 7 S.Ct. 1094 / 30 L.Ed. 995 / 1-19-1884
Milwaukee & N R Co v. Brooks Locomotive Works
Other / E MARINER / 1886 / 226 / 121 U.S. 430 / 7 S.Ct. 1094 / 30 L.Ed. 995 / 3-23-1887
Milwaukee & N R Co v. Brooks Locomotive Works
Brief for Defendant-In-Error / JAMES G JENKINS / 1886 / 226 / 121 U.S. 430 / 7 S.Ct. 1094 / 30 L.Ed. 995 / 4-12-1887
Milwaukee & N R Co v. Brooks Locomotive Works
Other / F C WINKLER / 1886 / 226 / 121 U.S. 430 / 7 S.Ct. 1094 / 30 L.Ed. 995 / 4-1-1886

Milwaukee & N R Co v. Brooks Locomotive Works U.S. Supreme Court Transcript of Record with Supporting Pleadings

Table of Contents

TRANSCRIPT OF RECORD.

SUPRÉME COURT OF THE UNITED STATES.

OCTOBER TERM, 1886.

No. 226.

THE MILWAUKEE AND NORTHERN RAILWAY COMPANY, PLAINTIFF IN ERROR,

vs.

THE BROOKS LOCOMOTIVE WORKS.

IN ERROR TO THE CIRCUIT COURT OF THE UNITED STATES FOR THE EASTERN DISTRICT OF WISCONSIN.

FILED JANUARY 19, 1884.

SUPREME COURT OF THE UNITED STATES.

OCTOBER TERM, 1886.

No. 226.

THE MILWAUKEE AND NORTHERN RAILWAY COMPANY, PLAINTIFF IN ERROR,

vs.

THE BROOKS LOCOMOTIVE WORKS.

IN ERROR TO THE CIRCUIT COURT OF THE UNITED STATES FOR THE EASTERN DISTRICT OF WISCONSIN.

INDEX.

JUDD & DETWEILER, PRINTERS, WASHINGTON.

1   Circuit Court of the United States for the Eastern District of Wisconsin.

UNITED STATES OF AMERICA, } *ss:*
Eastern District of Wisconsin,

At a special term of the circuit court of the United States for the eastern district of Wisconsin, begun and held at the city of Milwaukee, in said district, on the fourth Monday (being the twenty-third day) of July, A. D. 1883—present, the Honorable Charles E. Dyer, district judge, presiding; Edward Kurtz, clerk, and Henry Fink, marshal—among other the following proceedings were had, to wit:

THE BROOKS LOCOMOTIVE WORKS, Plaintiff,
vs.
THE MILWAUKEE & NORTHERN RAILWAY CO., Defendant;
The Wisconsin Central Railroad Company, Charles L. } At Law.
Colby, Edwin H. Abbot, and John A. Stewart &
Edwin H. Abbot, Trustees, Garnishees.

Be it remembered that heretofore, to wit, on the 7th day of July, A. D. 1879, came the above-named plaintiff, by its attorney, Mr. De Witt Davis, and filed its *præcipe* for a summons in the above-entitled cause, together with an affidavit in garnishment to be annexed thereto and bond for costs approved by the clerk, which *præcipe* and affidavit are as follows, to wit:

2   *Præcipe for Summons.*

United States Circuit Court, Eastern District of Wisconsin.

THE BROOKS LOCOMOTIVE WORKS
vs.
THE MILWAUKEE & NORTHERN RAILWAY COMPANY, Defendant;
The Wisconsin Central Railroad Company, Charles L. Colby,
Edwin H. Abbot, and John A. Stewart & Edwin H. Abbot as
Trustees, Garnishees.

Issue a summons in the above-entitled cause, returnable according to law.   DE WITT DAVIS,
                                            Pl'ff's Att'y.

To Edward Kurtz, clerk.

                Affidavit for Garnishment.

Circuit Court of the United States for the Eastern District of Wisconsin.

THE BROOKS LOCOMOTIVE WORKS, Plaintiff,
                    against
THE MILWAUKEE AND NORTHERN RAILWAY COMPANY, Defendant,
and The Wisconsin Central Railroad Company, Charles L. Colby,
Edwin Abbot, and John A. Stewart and Edwin H. Abbot as
Trustees, Garnishees.

3   EASTERN DISTRICT OF WISCONSIN, *ss.*

De Witt Davis, being duly sworn, says that he is the agent and
    1—226

attorney for the plaintiff in the above-entitled cause, and makes this affidavit on behalf of said plaintiff; that final judgment was rendered and docketed in the above-entitled action in said court, wherein said plaintiff was plaintiff and the above-named defendant was defendant, in favor of said plaintiff and against said defendant,

4 on the 30th day of November, A. D. 1875, for the sum of fifteen thousand three hundred and sixty-eight dollars and seventy-two cents, which said sum, with interest thereon, is now due thereupon from said defendant to the said plaintiff.

That said judgment has not been paid or satisfied, nor any part thereof, and that the action in which said judgment was rendered was founded upon express contract.

That an alias execution was duly issued in said cause upon said judgment against the property of said defendant on the 7th day of July, A. D. 1879; that said execution is in the hands of the marshal of said district and has not been returned, and that the same is returnable in sixty days from the said 7th day of July, 1879; that this affiant verily believes that the Wisconsin Central Railroad Company, a corporation duly created and existing under and by virtue of the laws of the State of Wisconsin, and having its principal office and place of business at Milwaukee, in said district; Charles L. Colby, Edwin H. Abbot, and John A. Stewart and said Edwin H. Abbot as trustees of and for the holders of the first-mortgage bonds of the Wisconsin Central Railroad Company, are indebted to or have property, real or personal, in their possession or under their control belonging to the said defendant in said execution, The Milwaukee and Northern Railway Company, and that said defendant, The Milwaukee and Northern Railway Company, has not property liable to execution sufficient to satisfy the said plaintiff's demand, and that the indebtedness or property herein mentioned are, to the best of the knowledge and belief of this affiant, not by law exempt from seizure or sale upon execution.

And this affiant further says that the indebtedness of the said John A. Stewart and Edwin H. Abbot as trustees of the holders of the first-mortgage bonds of the Wisconsin Central Railroad Company, as hereinbefore stated, is a joint indebtedness, and that the property so in their possession or under their control belonging to said defendant is held by them jointly, and that it is claimed that the liability of the said John A. Stewart and Edwin H. Abbot, trustees, as aforesaid, as garnishees herein, is a joint liability.

And this affiant further says that the said plaintiff is a citi-
5 zen of the State of New York and that said defendant, The Milwaukee and Northern Railway Company, and said garnishees, The Wisconsin Central Railroad Company, Charles L. Colby, and Edwin H. Abbot, are citizens of the State of Wisconsin, and that the property belonging to said defendant, The Milwaukee and Northern Railway Company, now in the possession or under the control of the said garnishees, or either of them, is within the State of Wisconsin and in the eastern district thereof, as this affiant is informed and believes.

DE WITT DAVIS.

Subscribed & sworn to before me this 7th day of July, A. D. 1879.
EDWARD KURTZ, *Clerk.*

Whereupon a summons issued as follows (with said affidavit annexed):

Summons.

Circuit Court of the United States for the Eastern District of Wisconsin.

THE BROOKS LOCOMOTIVE WORKS, Plaintiff,
against
THE MILWAUKEE AND NORTHERN RAILWAY COMPANY, Defendant, and The Wisconsin Central Railroad Company, Charles L. Colby, Edwin H. Abbot, and John A. Stewart and Edwin H. Abbot as Trustees, Garnishees.

6   The President of the United States of America to the said
     [SEAL.]   garnishees and each of them:

You are hereby summoned, pursuant to the annexed affidavit, as garnishees of the defendant, The Milwaukee and Northern Railway Company, and required, within twenty days after the service of this summons upon you, exclusive of the day of service, to answer according to law whether you are indebted to or have in your possession or under your control any property, real or personal, belonging to such defendant, and to serve a copy of your answer on the undersigned at Milwaukee, in the county of Milwaukee, in said district; and in case of your failure so to do you will be liable to further proceedings, according to law, of which the said defendant will also take notice.

The marshal of said district is hereby commanded to serve this summons and make due return thereto.

Witness the Honorable Morrison R. Waite, Chief Justice of the Supreme Court of the United States, at the city of Milwaukee, in the said eastern district of Wisconsin, this 7th day of July, in the year of our Lord one thousand eight hundred and seventy-nine, and of the Independence of the United States the 104th.

EDWARD KURTZ, *Clerk.*

DE WITT DAVIS,
Plaintiff's Attorney.

7   P. O. address, Milwaukee, Milwaukee county, Wisconsin.

Marshal's Return.

"Served on the within-named Wisconsin Central Railway Company, C. L. Colby, Edwin H. Abbot, and Edwin H. Abbot, trustee, garnishees, by showing this summons & affidavit and delivering a copy thereof to C. L. Colby, as pres'd't, and to Edwin H. Abbot, as sec'y & treas'r of said Wisc'n Cent'l R'y Co., and severally as individual garnishees, and Edwin H. Abbot as trustee for the bondholders of said Wisc'n Cent'l R'y Co., at Milwaukee this 7th day of July, A. D. 1879. John A. Stewart, trustee, not found. Also served on within-named defendant, The Milwaukee & Northern R. R. Company, by showing this summons & affidavit, & delivering a copy thereof to Angus Smith, vice-president thereof, at Milwaukee this 7th day of July, A. D. 1879.

"HENRY FINK, *Marshal*,
"By W. A. NOWELL, *Deputy*."

August 5, 1879.—This day came the defendant, The Milwaukee & Northern Railway Company, by its attorney, Mr. Mariner, and filed its answer, as follows:

Answer of Mil. & Northern Railway Co.

Circuit Court of the United States for the Eastern District of Wisconsin.

THE BROOKS LOCOMOTIVE WORKS, Plaintiff,
against
THE MILWAUKEE AND NORTHERN RAILWAY COMPANY, Defendant, and The Wisconsin Central Railroad Company, Charles L. Colby, Edwin H. Abbot, and John A. Stewart and Edwin H. Abbot, as Trustees, Garnishees.

And now comes the said Milwaukee and Northern Railway Company, defendant, by E. Mariner, its attorney, and in answer to said garnishment shows that the said Wisconsin Central Railroad Company Charles L. Colby, Edwin H. Abbot, and John A. Stewart and Edwin H. Abbot as trustees, were not, nor was any or either of them, indebted to the said Milwaukee and Northern Railway Company at the time of the service of the said garnishee process, and had not nor had either or any of them in his or its possession, nor under his or its control, any property, estate, or effects whatsoever of said Milwaukee and Northern Railway Company liable to such garnishment; that said Stewart and said Abbot, as trustees as aforesaid, were in possession of the railroad of said Milwaukee and Northern Railway Company, and operating the same under and by virtue of a lease theretofore made between said Edwin H. Abbot and John A. Stewart, as trustees, and James O. Spencer, receiver of the Milwaukee and Northern railway, appointed by said court in a certain cause therein pending in equity, in which Jesse Hoyt, trustee, was complainant, and this defendant, The Milwaukee and Northern Railway Company, The Wisconsin Central Railroad Company, and others were defendants, by the terms of which lease the rent was payable to said Spencer as such receiver; wherefore this defendant prays judgment that such garnishee proceeding may be dismissed with costs.

E. MARINER,
Defendants' Attorney.

EASTERN DISTRICT OF WISCONSIN, *ss :*

Be it remembered that on this 5th day of August, 1879, before me came Angus Smith, and made oath that he was the vice-president of said Milwaukee and Northern Railway Company; that he had heard read the foregoing answer; that the same was true of his own knowledge, except as to the matters therein stated upon information and belief, and that as to those matters he believed it to be true.

FRANK M. HOYT,
Notary Public, Milwaukee County, Wis.

9   May 12, 1880.—Answers of the Wisconsin Central Railroad Company, Charles L. Colby, and Edwin H. Abbot filed, as follows:

Answer of Wisconsin Central R. R. Co.

Circuit Court of the United States, Eastern District of Wisconsin.

THE BROOKS LOCOMOTIVE WORKS, Plaintiff,
against
THE MILWAUKEE AND NORTHERN RAILWAY COMPANY, Defendant, and The Wisconsin Central Railroad Company, Charles L. Colby, Edwin H. Abbot, and John A. Stewart and Edwin H. Abbot as Trustees, Garnishees.

EASTERN DISTRICT OF WISCONSIN, ⎱ ss:
City and County of Milwaukee, ⎰

Charles L. Colby, being first duly sworn, says that he is now, and for more than two years last past has been, president of the Wisconsin Central Railroad Company; that on the seventh day of July, A. D. 1879, he, as president of said Wisconsin Central Railroad Company, was served with a garnishee summons in the above-entitled action; that the said Wisconsin Central Railroad Company was then and is now in no manner and upon no account whatever, according to the best of his knowledge, information, and belief, indebted or under liability to the defendant, The Milwaukee and Northern
10   Railway Company, and that the said Wisconsin Central Railroad Company then had and now has in its possession or under its control no real estate and no personal property, effects, or credits of any description whatever belonging to said defendant, or in which it had any interest, to the best of deponent's knowledge, information, and belief, and, as this deponent verily believes, said Wisconsin Central Railroad Company is in nowise liable as garnishee in this action, and this affidavit is made by this deponent as president aforesaid of said Wisconsin Central Railroad Company and in its behalf.

CHAS. L. COLBY.

Subscribed and sworn to before me this sixteenth day of March, A. D. 1880.
[SEAL.]
K. KENT KENNAN,
Notary Public, Milwaukee County, Wisconsin.

Answer of Charles L. Colby.

Circuit Court of the United States, Eastern District of Wisconsin.

THE BROOKS LOCOMOTIVE WORKS, Plaintiff,
against
THE MILWAUKEE AND NORTHERN RAILWAY COMPANY, Defendant,
and The Wisconsin Central Railroad Company, Charles L. Colby,
Edwin H. Abbot, and John A. Stewart and Edwin H. Abbot as
Trustees, Garnishees.

11   EASTERN DISTRICT OF WISCONSIN, } ss :
      City and County of Milwaukee,

Charles L. Colby, being first duly sworn, says that on the seventh
day of July, A. D. 1879, he was served with a garnishee summons
in the above-entitled action; that he was then and is now in no
manner and upon no account whatever indebted or under liability
personally or in his individual capacity to the defendant, The Milwaukee and Northern Railway Company, and that he then had and
now has in his individual possession or under his individual control no real estate and no personal property, effects, or credits of any
description whatever belonging to said defendant, or in which the
said defendant has any interest, and he is in his individul capacity
in no manner liable as garnishee in this action.

CHAS. L. COLBY.

Subscribed and sworn to before me this sixteenth day of March,
A. D. 1880.

[SEAL.]   K. KENT KENNAN,
            Notary Public, Milwaukee County, Wisconsin.

Answer of Edwin H. Abbot.

Circuit Court of the United States, Eastern District of Wisconsin.

THE BROOKS LOCOMOTIVE WORKS, Plaintiff,
against
12   THE MILWAUKEE AND NORTHERN RAILWAY COMPANY, De-
      fendant, and The Wisconsin Central Railroad Company,
Charles L. Colby, Edwin H. Abbot, and John A. Stewart and
Edwin H. Abbot as Trustees, Garnishees.

EASTERN DISTRICT OF WISCONSIN, } ss :
City and County of Milwaukee,

Edwin H. Abbot, being first duly sworn, says that on the seventh
day of July, A. D. 1879, he was served with a garnishee summons
in the above-entitled action; that he was then and is now in no
manner and upon no account whatever indebted or under liability
personally or in his individual capacity to the defendant, The Milwaukee and Northern Railway Company, and that he then had and
now has in his individual possession or under his individual control
no real estate and no personal property, effects, or credits of any de-

scription whatever belonging to said defendant, or in which the said defendant has any interest, and he is in his individual capacity in no manner liable as garnishee in this action.

EDWIN H. ABBOT.

Subscribed and sworn to before me this sixteenth day of March, A. D. 1880.

[SEAL.]

K. KENT KENNAN,
Notary Public, Milwaukee County, Wisconsin.

13 And same day (May 12, 1880) answer of Edwin H. Abbot, in behalf of John A. Stewart and Edwin H. Abbot, as trustees and garnishees, filed as follows:

Answer of Edwin H. Abbot in Behalf of Himself & John A. Stewart, Trustees, as Garnishees.

Circuit Court of the United States, Eastern District of Wisconsin.

THE BROOKS LOCOMOTIVE WORKS, Plaintiff,
against
THE MILWAUKEE AND NORTHERN RAILWAY COMPANY, Defendant, and The Wisconsin Central Railroad Company, Charles L. Colby, Edwin H. Abbot, and John A. Stewart and Edwin H. Abbot as Trustees, Garnishees.

EASTERN DISTRICT OF WISCONSIN, }
City and County of Milwaukee, } *ss:*

Edwin H. Abbot, being first duly sworn, says that on the seventh day of July, A. D. 1879, he and the defendant, John A. Stewart, of the city, county, and State of New York, were summoned as garnishees, in their joint capacity as trustees of the Wisconsin Central railroad; that they were then the trustees of the Wisconsin Central railroad and in possession thereof, under and according to the terms of their indenture of trust and mortgage of said railroad dated the
14 first day of July, A. D. 1871; that said Stewart then resided and was and still is beyond the jurisdiction of this court, and that this affiant now answers jointly for said trustees in this action; that the garnishee summons in said action was served upon this affiant on the aforesaid seventh day of July, A. D. 1879, upon the ground, as he is informed, that this affiant was jointly liable with said John A. Stewart, as trustee aforesaid, upon some alleged indebtedness of said trustees to said Milwaukee and Northern Railway Company. Said Edwin H. Abbot, in behalf of himself and said Stewart, trustees as aforesaid, now answers to said garnishee process: That this affiant is informed and believes and therefore avers:

First. That the Wisconsin Central Railroad Company, on or about the eighth day of November, A. D. 1873, executed with said Milwaukee and Northern Railway Company a lease of the Milwaukee and Northern railway, so called, a copy of which is hereto annexed, and marked Exhibit "A."

Second. That said Wisconsin Central Railroad Company thereafter, on or about the first day of December, A. D. 1873, entered into and upon and took possession of said Milwaukee and Northern railway under said lease; that thereafter said Milwaukee and Northern Railway Company and said Wisconsin Central Railroad Company executed a certain supplemental agreement, dated the first day of June, A. D. 1875, copy of which is hereto annexed and marked Exhibit " B."

Third. That thereafter said companies executed a certain agreement, dated the tenth day of October, A. D. 1876, copy of which is hereto annexed and marked Exhibit " C."

Fourth. That thereafter, to wit, on or about the eighth day of January, A. D. 1878, as this affiant is informed and believes, a certain notice was served upon said railroad company purporting to describe an alleged assignment of said lease to one Jesse Hoyt, trustee, copy of which is hereto annexed and marked Exhibit " D;" but this affiant is ignorant as to the truth of the statements contained in said notice, and whether said assignment was ever made as therein stated, and, if ever made as alleged, what its terms and contents are, 15   and whether the same was made upon any consideration, and, if so, what; but this affiant is informed and believes that said Jesse Hoyt was then and there, and ever since has been, and still is the president of the Milwaukee and Northern Railway Company.

Fifth. That, thereafter, on or about the third day of January, A. D. 1879, this affiant and John A. Stewart, as trustees aforesaid, lawfully and under and by virtue of the provisions of their indenture of trust and mortgage of the Wisconsin Central railroad, hereinbefore referred to, entered upon and took possession, pursuant to the terms of their trust, of the property covered by that mortgage, and thenceforth operated and are now operating the Wisconsin Central railroad in fulfilment of said trust and of their duty as said trustees; that when they took possession, as aforesaid, they found said Wisconsin Central Railroad Company was operating the Milwaukee and Northern railway under the lease and agreements aforesaid; that said trustees refused to recognize and accept said lease in any manner or form, and refused to ratify the same or to operate said Milwaukee and Northern railway under the same, and never did recognize, accept, or ratify said lease or operate said railway under it, but declined absolutely to assume any obligation whatever under that lease, and so notified the Milwaukee and Northern Railway Company and said Jesse Hoyt, as he was the president of said railway company, and the surviving trustee under its first mortgage and bonds, and the trustee under the lease of the Milwaukee and Northern Railway Company to the Wisconsin Central Railroad Company, and the assignee of said lease named in said notice of said alleged assignment thereof, and served upon said Hoyt a certain notice in writing, copy of which is hereto annexed and marked Exhibit E, and also served upon one Angus Smith, as he was the vice-president of said Milwaukee and Northern Railway Company, and the agent in Milwaukee of said Jesse Hoyt, a copy of said notice on the same day, to wit, the eleventh day of January, A. D. 1879.

Sixth. That said trustees Stewart and Abbot remained in possession, as aforesaid, of the Milwaukee and Northern railway until the first day of May, A. D. 1879, without objection from 16, any of the parties interested in said railway, and during the intervening period received the earnings thereof; that subsequently, on the twenty-third day of July, A. D. 1879, upon an accounting together, it was agreed by and between said Stewart and Abbot, as trustees as aforesaid, and said Jesse Hoyt, as president of the Milwaukee and Northern Railway Company, and as trustee of the Milwaukee and Northern Railway Company, and surviving trustee under its first mortgage and bonds, and trustee under its lease of its railway to the Wisconsin Central Railroad Company, and assignee of said lease under alleged assignment thereof from said Milwaukee and Northern Railway Company, and in any and every other capacity wherein said Hoyt represented said railway, said Hoyt being then and there the president of said Milwaukee and Northern Railway Company, that the sum of twenty-eight thousand two hundred fifty-eight and forty-four one-hundredths dollars ($28,258.44) was the amount and the only amount payable by said trustees Stewart and Abbot to the party lawfully entitled to receive the same out of the moneys received by said trustees' Stewart and Abbot from the operation of the Milwaukee and Northern railway since the third day of January, A. D. 1879, to the first day of May, A. D. 1879, in full settlement of all account thereof between said trustees and the parties interested in said railway and in full settlement for said trustees', Stewart and Abbot, operation of said railway during said period; that said sum of twenty-eight thousand two hundred fifty-eight and $\frac{44}{100}$ dollars ($28,258.44) was the reasonable and fair rental, and the whole amount properly to be paid by said trustees for the use and occupation of the railroad of the Milwaukee and Northern Railway Company while so in possession of the said trustees Stewart and Abbot; that this sum was in possession of said trustees Stewart and Abbot in their capacity of trustees, as aforesaid, at the date of the service aforesaid upon them of the garnishee summons in the above-entitled action; and the said Stewart and Abbot, being in doubt as to whether the facts and circumstances aforesaid, which are fully and truthfully set forth, cast any liability as garnishees 17 upon them, have answered fully and hereby submit the question of their liability to the court.

(Signed)   EDWIN H. ABBOT,
                                    Trustee as Aforesaid.

Subscribed and sworn to before me this sixteenth day of March, A. D. 1880.

[SEAL.]   K. KENT KENNAN,
                         Notary Public, Milwaukee County, Wisconsin.

EXHIBIT "A."

This indenture of lease, made this eighth day of November, A. D. 1873, by and between The Milwaukee and Northern Railway Company, party of the first part, and The Wisconsin Central Railroad Company, party of the second part—

Witnesseth : That the first party, in consideration of the agreements of the second party hereinafter contained, has let, demised, and leased, and by these presents does let, demise, and lease, unto the second party all that part of the railroad constructed by the first party extending from its terminus in Milwaukee county to Green Bay, together with the branch to Menasha, all in the State of Wisconsin, and all its tracks, depots and depot grounds, rights of way, bridges, side tracks, turn-tables, water-tanks, engine houses, shops, and buildings, and all its motive power and rolling-stock of every description, its iron rails, fish-plates, spikes, tools, implements, railroad materials and supplies of every description now on hand for the construction and repair of said railroad, and all its property of every sort and description, rights, liberties, franchises, and privileges belonging to said first party in any way appertaining to the demised premises, subject to a certain mortgage executed by the first party to Jesse Hoyt and A. Warren Greenleaf, trustees, to secure payment of its first-mortgage bonds, which are issued, or to be issued, at the rate of eighteen thousand dollars per mile and

18   no more on said road, dated December 1st, A. D. 1870, and recorded in the office of the secretary of state of the State of Wisconsin. A schedule of the demised property is hereto annexed and marked A :

To have and to hold the same for and during the term of nine hundred and ninety-nine years from and after the thirtieth day of November, A. D. eighteen hundred and seventy-three, in undisturbed possession, use, and control unto the second party, its successors and assigns, provided the agreements, covenants, and stipulations made herein by the second party are faithfully performed, and until breach, if any, thereof by the second party, its successors or assigns.

Yielding and paying rent therefor as follows, to wit: In and for each year of said term wherein the gross earnings received from the demised premises, as hereinafter set forth, shall exceed the sum of one million dollars, thirty per cent. of said gross earnings; and in and for each year of said term wherein said gross earnings shall exceed eight hundred thousand dollars, but not exceed one million dollars, thirty-three per centum of said gross earnings; and in and for each year of said term wherein said gross earnings shall be less than eight hundred thousand dollars, thirty-five per cent. of said gross earnings. Upon the first day of February, A. D. eighteen hundred and seventy-four, the second party shall state to the first party an account, as nearly exact as is practicable, of the gross earnings received from and upon the demised premises during the month of December, A. D. eighteen hundred and seventy-three, and shall, semi-annually, state an exact account of said gross earnings for the six months ending May thirty-first and November thirtieth, as soon thereafter as the same can be made up, and within ten months thereafter in any event. Like accounts, approximately made, shall be stated to the first party on the first day of every month of and for the business of the month next but one preceding; and upon said first day of February and the first day of each following month during said term the second party shall pay the amount of rent so approximated, at the rate of thirty-five per cent., until facts show that the earnings will warrant a lower rate, for the month next but one preceding, 19 to such trustee as shall be from time to time jointly selected by the parties hereto upon the trust to keep the same until the next installment of interest is due upon the bonds issued by the first party under their first mortgage, and then to apply the same, or so much thereof as shall be necessary, to the payment of said interest when and as payable, and, if any surplus remain after payment of said interest, to pay the same to the first party, its successors and assigns, unless said surplus or some part thereof is due to the second party for advances, as is hereinafter provided, made to or for the benefit of the first party to pay said interest, and if said surplus, or any part thereof, is so due, then to second party, as hereinafter provided, so much as is due for said advances and interest. But said rent shall not be paid over to the first party until and unless all matured interest has been paid on said bonds and all advances made by the second party on said interest account repaid to said second party, but in every case so much thereof as shall be necessary for that purpose shall be applied, first, to said matured interest, and, second, to the reimbursement of said advances and interest thereon, and the remainder paid over to the first party. All accounts shall be exactly balanced upon the semi-annual statements aforesaid. Until otherwise jointly agreed the Wisconsin Marine and Fire Insurance Company Bank is appointed trustee aforesaid, and every such trustee shall be required to give security, whenever either party shall so request in writing, in such manner and amount as the parties hereto may agree upon, or any court having jurisdiction in the premises determine.

Gross earnings herein shall be taken to mean gross receipts less all taxes; and it is agreed that all taxes shall be deducted from the gross receipts and paid by the second party before computation of rent on gross earnings.

And the parties hereto covenant with each other as follows, to wit:

First. The Milwaukee and Northern Railway Company covenants that it is lawfully empowered to make this lease, and that it will 20 maintain and protect the second party in quiet and peaceable use, possession, and enjoyment of the demised premises, and will warrant and defend the same to the second party during the term aforesaid, or until possession taken for breach, if any, by the second party of its agreements and covenants.

Second. The first party also covenants that it will complete certain constructions, repairs, and improvements enumerated in schedule marked "B," hereto annexed.

Third. The first party also covenants that it will assign to the second party, or, at its election, carry out in the name of the first party, but for the benefit, at the expense, and under the direction of

the second party, all outstanding contracts, undertakings, agreements, and connections with other railroads and individuals, so far
as the same are assignable and the second party elects, which the
first party has made for the operation and improvement of the demised premises.

Fourth. The first party further covenants that it will pay at their
maturity, either by a new issue of bonds not larger in amount, nor
at a higher rate of interest, nor at a greater rate per mile, than its
present first-mortgage bonds, or in such other manner as it may
elect without increasing in any way its indebtedness beyond eighteen
thousand dollars per mile upon the demised railroad at eight per
centum per annum interest its present first-mortgage bonds, and that it
will pay all interest when and as the same is due upon said first-mortgage bonds, and forever hold the second party harmless therefrom,
and will not issue any more bonds under its present mortgage beyond the amount of eighteen thousand dollars per mile upon the
demised premises, and will not in any way make, create, or suffer
any other lien or incumbrance whatever upon said demised premises during the term of this agreement without the consent of the
second party.

Fifth. The first party further covenants that it will issue bonds
under a new mortgage, or otherwise provide means for laying an
additional track whenever the second party shall request, and a
commission composed of the presidents of both roads and a
third person jointly selected by them shall certify that the business of the road requires a second track for its accommodation, and
said bonds shall be negotiated and the proceeds applied under
21   the direction of the second party, and the second party
shall, if desired, provide for the payment of interest thereon in
the same manner as is provided in this indenture in regard to the
first-mortgage bond snow outstanding. The first party also agrees
that whenever and if the first party takes possession of the demised
premises it will pay the second party the fair value of all buildings and
permanent improvements made by the second party upon the demised premises and will allow the second party to remove all its
own motive power and rolling-stock.

Sixth. The Wisconsin Central Railroad Company agrees to accept the demise and lease of the demised premises, and to operate
the same and maintain in first-class condition the railroad of the
first party in connection with and as part of its own road, and to
keep the same, including all fixtures, tools, implements, and rolling-
stock, in good repair, and do all of its own business which it can
control over the road of the first party, and use its best efforts to develop the business of both roads alike and make the road of the first
party its trunk line to Milwaukee. But this agreement is not intended to preclude it from extending its own road, by lease or
otherwise, to Portage city and to Manitowoc.

Seventh. The second party further agrees to keep full and true
books of account, showing the business done upon the demised
premises, and will credit the first party with its *pro rata* share of
the gross earnings upon said demised premises, to wit, the same pro-

portion thereof which the distance [the] freight and passengers are transported over the road of the first party bears to the whole distance they are transported by the second party, and will allow the president, or other officer of the first part duly authorized for that purpose, at all reasonable times to inspect the said books, and will furnish them with full information to ascertain the gross earnings and the proportion thereof to which the first party is entitled, and will allow them to examine the road and rolling-stock and demised premises, and will keep the same in substantially as good working order and repair as they are in when delivered to the second party.

Eighth. The second party also covenants to pay the rent
22 hereinbefore reserved when and as payable, and also covenants, if the rent paid to the trustees aforesaid in any six months previous to the payment of interest on the said first-mortgage bonds is not enough to pay the whole interest then maturing, to advance so much money as may be necessary to take up the balance of the coupons for interest as they become due and payable, and to take them up; and it is expressly agreed between the parties to these presents that for all sums so advanced the second party shall hold said coupons as a lien, and the same is hereby made and constituted a lien on the rent hereby reserved and on all property hereby demised and leased prior to and superior to all other liens except the said mortgage until the same be fully reimbursed with interest at eight per centum per annum out of the said rent or otherwise by the first party. It is also agreed that any surplus of rent which appears upon the semi-annual adjustments of accounts shall be paid to the second party, so far as may be needed to cover any advances and interest thereon made to protect the coupons aforesaid, and that only the residue of said surplus, if any, shall be paid to the first party.

Ninth. It is further jointly agreed that, if the second party fails or neglects for the space of six months after written demand made by the first party to perform any of its covenants and agreements herein contained, then it shall be lawful for the first party, in addition to all other remedies at law or in equity, to enter upon the demised premises and repossess itself of the same; and the second party covenants peaceably to surrender the same upon said entry.

In witness whereof the parties hereto have caused these presents to be signed by Angus Smith, vice-president of the Milwaukee and Northern Railway Company, for and in behalf of said company, and by Gardner Colby, president of the Wisconsin Central Railroad Company, for and in behalf of said company, they being thereunto lawfully authorized so to do, and the seals of said companies to
23 be hereto affixed, this eighth day of November, A. D. 1873, in the city of Milwaukee and State of Wisconsin.

(Signed)   THE MILWAUKEE AND NORTHERN
            RAILWAY COMPANY,
         By ANGUS SMITH, *Vice-President.* [SEAL.]
(Signed)   WISCONSIN CENTRAL R. R. CO.,
         By GARDNER COLBY, *President.* [SEAL.]

In presence of—
  O. H. WALDO.

SCHEDULE B.

As provided for in the lease of the Milwaukee and Northern Railway Company to the Wisconsin Central Railroad Company, dated November 8th, A. D. 1873—

The Milwaukee and Northern Railway Company agree to fully complete the depot at Greenleaf station and the depot at Ledgeville before the first day of January, A. D. 1874, and to fully complete the fencing on the whole line of railway to Menasha and Green Bay on or before the first of July, A. D. 1874.

Agree to connect side track at Lathams with main track on north end before January 1st, 1874, and to complete the engine-house and water tank at Green Bay on or before January 1st, 1874.

The said company also agrees to build at Green Bay a depot similar to that at Depere, and to extend track to north side of block seven (7) before July 1st, 1874, and to extend tracks in Menasha to the river above the dam before the close of 1873, and also in the rear of buildings on the water power before the first of June, 1874, if the Wisconsin Central Railroad Company so elect.

Agreed to on behalf of the Milwaukee and Northern Railway Company.

    `(Signed)   ·   E. B. GREENLEAF,
                                Gen'l Manager.

Agreed to on behalf of the Wisconsin Central Railroad Company.

24   EXHIBIT "B."

Supplementary agreement made this first day of June, A. D. eighteen hundred and seventy-five, by and between the Milwaukee and Northern Railway Company and the Wisconsin Central Railroad Company.

Whereas on the eighth day of November, A. D. eighteen hundred and seventy-three, the Milwaukee and Northern Railway Company, party of the first part, and the Wisconsin Central Railroad Company, party of the second part, executed a certain indenture of lease of the Milwaukee and Northern railroad and other property ; and whereas certain modifications of said lease have been mutually by said companies agreed:

Now, therefore, said companies, for themselves, their successors, and assigns, respectively do hereby, in addition to the stipulations of said lease and in modification thereof, so far as those stipulations are inconsistent herewith, agree as follows, to wit:

First. In lieu of the rent reserved in lease and of all advances of money to take up the interest coupons of the Milwaukee and Northern Railway Company, as provided in said lease, the Wisconsin Central Railroad Company shall pay, and the Milwaukee and Northern Railway Company shall accept, for and during the space of three years from and after the first day of June, A. D. eighteen hundred and seventy-five (1875), the amount of forty per cent. of the gross earnings received from the demised premises, and, after the expiration of said three years and during the remainder of the term, the rent shall be paid as reserved in said lease if the rent so reserved is sufficient to pay said coupons, but if not sufficient to pay said coupons, then the Wisconsin Central Railroad Company shall pay, and the Milwaukee and Northern Railway Company shall accept, in full satisfaction of rent for the demised premises, such part of said gross earnings, not exceeding in any event forty per cent. thereof, as shall be sufficient to pay said coupons, all accounts being settled exactly, and all liabilities and obligations between the two companies being adjusted and discharged by and upon the semi-annual statements provided in said lease, and on the 25   thirty-first day of May and the thirtieth day of November in each year, and said semi-annual statements being accepted by each company as final adjustments of all claims for rent of the demised premises to the respective dates thereof.

Second. Taxes, from and after the first day of January, A. D. eighteen hundred and eighty (1880), shall not be deducted from the gross receipts before computation of rent for the demised premises, but shall thenceforward be borne and paid by the lessee as part of the operating expenses.

Third. The Milwaukee and Northern Railway Company hereby agrees to perform prior to December first, A. D. eighteen hundred and seventy-six (1876), all its agreements in reference to the demised premises which are at this date unfulfilled, and to complete without unnecessary delay the various structures which are on its part contemplated to be built under provisions of said lease and schedules, and also hereby agrees that if the same be not finished prior to the first day of December, A. D. 1876, then the lessee is hereby authorized to complete the same forthwith at the expense of the lessor and to apply to this purpose, so far as is necessary for such completion, any surplus rent, after payment of the coupons aforesaid, which shall be then or thereafter earned.

Fourth. The Milwaukee and Northern Railway Company, in consideration of the increased rental and agreements aforesaid on the part of the Wisconsin Central Railroad Company, hereby releases the Wisconsin Central Railroad Company from any and all obligation to hereafter make any advances of money to take up the interest coupons of the Milwaukee and Northern Railway Company, as stipulated in said lease, and also from any and every obligation and liability arising out of any previous neglect to make said advances hitherto due and payable under terms of said lease, and also from any and every obligation to pay any money under said lease and any provision thereof in the nature of rent and advances to or for the benefit of the Milwaukee and Northern Railway Company, except the proportion of gross earnings (not exceeding in any event forty per cent. thereof) which is herein agreed, when and as the same is payable under terms of this agreement and said lease.

26   Fifth. If any difference of opinion arise as to the performance by either party of its covenants contained in said lease and in this agreement said difference shall be submitted to three competent arbitrators, who shall be jointly selected by the parties,

or, in default of such selection within sixty days after written request therefor, shall be appointed on the application of either party, after ten days' notice in writing to the other party, by any judge of the circuit court of the United States having for the time being jurisdiction in this district or of some United States court succeeding said court in said district. And it is further agreed that the written award of said arbitrators, or a majority of the same, made after due notice to and hearing of both parties and their witnesses, shall have the legal effect of an award.

Sixth. All the provisions of said lease, except so far as the same are herein expressly modified or changed, are hereby by each of said companies ratified and confirmed, and all causes of action for breach of any agreement therein contained, which have arisen from its date of execution until this day, are hereby mutually waived and forever released by and between said companies.

In witness whereof the parties hereto have caused these presents to be signed respectfully by Angus Smith, vice-president of the Milwaukee and Northern Railway Company, for and in behalf of the Milwaukee and Northern Railway Company, and by Gardner Colby, president of the Wisconsin Central Railroad Company, for and in behalf of the Wisconsin Central Railroad Company, they being thereunto lawfully authorized so to do, and the seals of the said companies to be hereto affixed this first day of June, A. D. eighteen hundred and seventy-five, in the city of Milwaukee and State of Wisconsin.

(Signed)   THE MILWAUKEE AND NORTHERN
                     RAILWAY COMPANY,
[SEAL.]   By ANGUS SMITH, *Vice-President.*
(Signed)   THE WISCONSIN CENTRAL RAIL-
                     ROAD COMPANY,
[SEAL.]   By GARDNER COLBY, *President.*

In presence of—
(Signed)   E. MARINER.
                     L. S. DIXON.

27   STATE OF WISCONSIN,   } ss:
                County of Milwaukee,

MILWAUKEE, *June 2d,* 1875.

Personally appeared Gardner Colby, president of the Wisconsin Central Railroad Company, and Angus Smith, vice-president of the Milwaukee and Northern Railway Company, and severally acknowledged the foregoing instrument to be the free act and deed of their respective corporations.

Before me—
[SEAL.]   (Signed)   F. W. WEBSTER,
                                                       Notary Public.

Exhibit " C."

Agreement made this tenth day of October, A. D. eighteen hundred and seventy-six, by and between the Milwaukee and Northern Railway Company; Jesse Hoyt and A. Warren Greenleaf, trustees; James Ludington, Guido Pfister, Angus Smith, and Jesse Hoyt, parties of the first part, and the Wisconsin Central Railroad Company, party of the second part:

Whereas, on the eighth day of November, A. D. eighteen hundred and seventy-three, the Milwaukee and Northern Railway Company executed to and with the Wisconsin Central Railroad Company an indenture of lease of the Milwaukee and Northern railroad, wherein the Wisconsin Marine and Fire Insurance Company Bank was appointed a trustee for certain purposes therein declared;

And whereas, on the first day of June, A. D. eighteen hundred and seventy-five, said corporations executed a supplemental agreement modifying said lease, and subsequently, on the same day, executed an additional agreement, whereby Jesse Hoyt, of the city of New York, was appointed temporary trustee under said lease so as aforesaid modified, for the period of twelve months, which period has now expired;

And whereas said Jesse Hoyt and A. Warren Greenleaf,
28   trustees of the first mortgage and bonds of the Milwaukee
        and Northern Railway Company, have heretofore instituted
against said company a suit in equity in the circuit court of the United States for the eastern district of Wisconsin for the foreclosure of said mortgage and bonds, and are now entitled, at their option, to take a decree against said Milwaukee and Northern Railway Company and evict said company from said railway and all other property covered by said mortgage and lease;

And whereas said James Ludington has heretofore instituted against the Milwaukee and Northern Railway Company a suit in the circuit court of Milwaukee county, in the State of Wisconsin, wherein he has obtained a judgment of foreclosure and sale against said company;

And whereas, on the 27th day of December, A. D. eighteen hundred and seventy-five, all the franchises of the Milwaukee and Northern Railway Company and all its property, records, and writings, together with said lease of said railway, was in pursuance of said judgment sold at public auction by the sheriff of said Milwaukee county;

And whereas Guido Pfister, Angus Smith, James Ludington, and Jesse Hoyt allege some claim or title, legal or equitable, jointly or severally, in and to the premises, under and by virtue of said sale, or otherwise;

And whereas all the parties interested in the premises desire the appointment of a trustee under said lease so as aforesaid modified, without prejudice to the legal rights of either party in the premises:

Now, therefore, the parties of the first part severally declare that no person or corporation not now joined in this agreement is, to the best of their knowledge, information, and belief, in any way interested, or asserts any rights, title, or interest in and to the premises, or any part thereof, and they severally request the party of the second part to assent to the appointment of Jesse Hoyt as trustee under said lease so as aforesaid modified, and hereby declare that

29   any and all receipts given by said Hoyt for any and all moneys to him paid by the lessee on account of the rental reserved in said lease so as aforesaid modified shall be a full quittance to the lessee therefor and an absolute bar in favor of said lessee against any and all persons whatsoever claiming the same, and the said parties of the first part jointly and severally covenant to hold said lessee harmless against any and all claim at any time hereafter made by any person or corporation whatsoever as to the moneys so paid to said Hoyt as trustee.

And all the parties hereto do hereby agree and consent that Jesse Hoyt, of the city, county, and State of New York, be, and hereby is, appointed trustee under said lease and supplemental agreement and shall so continue until ninety days after written notice shall have been given by any one or more of the parties herein named to said Hoyt of their desire to appoint a new trustee in his place, and that said Hoyt shall, at the expiration of ninety days after said notice has been given, cease to be such trustee, whereupon all the rights of the several parties hereto shall be the same as if this agreement had never been made.

And Jesse Hoyt hereby accepts said trust and agrees that during the time he shall be trustee as aforesaid either party to said lease may, in the name of, but without any expense to, said Hoyt, use his name as trustee in any legal proceedings which said party may desire to institute in order to obtain the decision of the United States circuit court upon the construction of said lease or administration of said trust.

In testimony whereof the Milwaukee and Northern Railway Company has caused these presents to be sealed with its common seal and to be signed by Jesse Hoyt, its president, for and in behalf of said company, and said Jesse Hoyt and A. Warren Greenleaf, trustees; Guido Pfister, Angus Smith, James Ludington, and Jesse Hoyt have hereto set their hands and seals, and said Wisconsin Central

30   Railroad Company has caused these presents to be sealed with its corporate seal and to be signed by Charles L. Colby, its vice-president, for and in behalf of said company, the day and year above written.

MILWAUKEE AND NORTHERN
RAILWAY CO.,

[SEAL.]   (Signed)   By JESSE HOYT, *President.*
           (Signed)   JESSE HOYT, *Trustee.*   [SEAL.]
                       A. W. GREENLEAF, *Trustee.*   [SEAL.]
                       JAMES LUDINGTON, *Trustee.*   [SEAL.]

EXHIBIT "D."

MILWAUKEE, WIS., *Jan. 8th*, 1878.

The Wisconsin Central Railway Company—Charles L. Colby, president.

DEAR SIR: You will please take notice that the lease between the Milwaukee and Northern Railway Company and your company, and all modifications thereof, and all rents due and to grow due thereon, and all the covenants in such lease and the modifications thereof have been assigned to us upon the trusts contained in the mortgage deed to us to secure the first-mortgage bands, and that you are expected to pay over the rents to Mr. Jesse Hoyt, as you have heretofore paid them, such assignment being intended merely as further security for said bonds and not to disturb the relations of the parties to such lease and modifications.

Yours, etc..   JESSE HOYT AND
               A. WARREN GREENLEAF,
(Signed)   By E. MARINER, *Their Attorney.*

EXHIBIT "E."

NEW YORK CITY, N. Y., *Jan'y 11th*, '79.

Jesse Hoyt, Esq., president of the Milwaukee and Northern
31   Railway Company, and surviving trustee under its first
      mortgage and bonds, and trustee under its lease of its railway
to the Wisconsin Central Railroad Company, and assignee of said lease under assignment thereof.

DEAR SIR: We beg to inform you that on the third day of January current we, as trustees under and by virtue of the provisions of the first mortgage of the Wisconsin Central Railroad Company, entered upon and took possession of the property covered by that mortgage, and are now operating the Wisconsin Central railroad.

We find that said company was operating the Milwaukee and Northern railway under a lease. We are not sufficiently informed upon the subject to warrant us in assuming any obligation under that lease. We therefore notify you that we decline to assume, affirm, or in any way ratify that lease. We wish, however, not to interfere in any way with the welfare of that railway; and, unless you otherwise elect, will continue for the present to operate the same temporarily for such compensation as that service may be fairly worth, and, as far as is necessary, but not in excess of its earnings, to repair the same as the Wisconsin Central Railroad Company was doing, and also to permit the business of the Wisconsin Central Railroad Company to be done as heretofore over that railway. We suggest that you arrange for an early personal interview with us, at which you will make known to us your wishes, and confer with a view to a more permanent arrangement.

We are ready to submit to the parties in interest any proposition which yourself and we are jointly able to recommend.

We are, very respectfully, your obedient servants,
(Signed)   JOHN A. STEWART,
               EDWIN H. ABBOT,
                              Trustees.

32   And same day (May 12, 1880) came the plaintiff, by its attorney, and filed notice that it takes issue on the answer of the defendant, Milwaukee & Northern Railway Company, and also filed notice that it takes issue upon the answer of John A. Stewart and Edwin H. Abbot, trustees, as garnishees, which notices are as follows:

Notice of Taking Issue on Answer of Defendant.

Circuit Court of the United States for the Eastern District of Wisconsin.

THE BROOKS LOCOMOTIVE WORKS, Plaintiff,
against

THE MILWAUKEE AND NORTHERN RAILWAY COMPANY, Defendant, and The Wisconsin Central Railroad Company, Charles L. Colby, Edwin H. Abbot, and John A. Stewart and Edwin H. Abbot, Trustees, Garnishees.

To the Milwaukee and Northern Railway Company, Defendant:

You will please to take notice that the above-named plaintiff has elected and hereby does elect to take issue on your answer to the garnishee summons served in the above-entitled action on the unsigned, the plaintiff's attorney therein, on the 8th day of August, A. D. 1879, and that the said plaintiff will maintain the said above-named garnishees to be liable as garnishees of the above-named defendant in the above-entitled action notwithstanding your said answer.

Dated Milwaukee, August 19th, A. D. 1879.

DE WITT DAVIS,
Plff's Att'y.

33   Endorsed as follows: Due service of a copy of the within notice admitted this 19th day of August, A. D. 1879. E. Mariner, def'ts' att'y.

Notice of Taking Issue on Answer of Stewart & Abbot, Trustees, as Garnishees.

Circuit Court of the United States, Eastern District of Wisconsin.

THE BROOKS LOCOMOTIVE WORKS, Plaintiff,
against

THE MILWAUKEE AND NORTHERN RAILWAY COMPANY, Defendant, and The Wisconsin Central Railroad Company, Charles L. Colby, Edwin H. Abbot, and John Stewart and Edwin H. Abbot, as Trustee, Garnishees.

GENTLEMEN: You will please to take notice that the above-named plaintiff hereby elects to take issue on your answer to the garnishee summons in the above-entitled action, and will maintain you to be liable as garnishee of the above-named defendant, The Milwaukee and Northern Railway Company, in the above-entitled action, notwithstanding your said answer.

Yours, &c., DAVIS AND RIESS,
Plaintiff's Attorneys.

To John Stewart and Edwin H. Abbot, as trustees, garnishees.

Endorsed as follows : Due service of within notice admitted August 28th, A. D. 1879. John A. Stewart & Edwin H. Abbot,
34   trustees, by E. H. Abbot. May 15, 1883. Deposition of E. H. Abbot received from Hugh Ryan, U. S. com'r, & filed.

And afterwards, to wit, at a stated term of said court begun and held according to law at the city of Milwaukee on the first Monday of January, A. D. 1883, and on the ninety-fourth day thereof, to wit, on the 17th day of May, A. D. 1883—present, the Hon. John M. Harlan, associate justice of the Supreme Court of the United States, assigned to this circuit, presiding, and the Hon. Charles E. Dyer, district judge—the following proceedings were had, to wit:

Trial.

BROOKS LOCOMOTIVE WORKS
vs.
THE MILWAUKEE & NORTHERN RAILWAY Co., Defendant, and The Wisconsin Central Railroad Company, Charles L. Colby, Edwin H. Abbot, and John A. Stewart & Edwin H. Abbot as Trustees, Garnishees.   } At law.

This day came the parties, by their counsel, Messrs. Jenkins, Wegg, and Shepard appearing for the plaintiff, and Mr. Mariner for the defendant, The Milwaukee & Northern Railway Company, and Mr. H. M. Finch for the garnishees, John A. Stewart and Edwin H. Abbot, trustees, and the issues between the plaintiff and said defendant and garnishees came on to be tried, when the said
35   parties entered into a written agreement, as herein filed, waiving a jury and consenting that the said issues be tried by the court as follows, to wit:

Stipulation Waiving a Jury.

Circuit Court of the United States, Eastern District of Wisconsin.
BROOKS LOCOMOTIVE WORKS, Plaintiff,
vs.
MILWAUKEE & NORTHERN RAILWAY COMPANY, Defendant, and The Wisconsin Central Railroad Company, John A. Stewart, and Edwin H. Abbot as Trustees, &c., *et al.*, Garnishees.

It is hereby stipulated that the issues in the above-entitled matter be tried by the court, and that a jury is hereby expressly waived.

Dated May 16th, 1883.

DE WITT DAVIS,
Plaintiff's Attorney.

FINCHES, LYNDE & MILLER,
*Attorneys for Garnishees, John A. Stewart &
Edwin H. Abbot, as Trustees.*

E. MARINER,
Att'y for the Milwaukee & Northern Railway Company.

Whereupon the court proceeded to try said issues, and the trial not being concluded the same was adjourned until to-morrow morning.

MAY 18, 1883.

This day came the parties, by their counsel, and the trial of the issue herein by the court was resumed, and being concluded the court held the same under consideration.

36   And afterwards, to wit, on the ninety-seventh day of said term, to wit, on the 21st day of May, A. D. 1883—present, the Hon. John M. Harlan, associate justice of the Supreme Court of the United States, assigned to this circuit, presiding, and the Hon. Charles E. Dyer, district judge—the following proceedings were had, to wit:

THE BROOKS LOCOMOTIVE WORKS
vs.
THE MILWAUKEE & NORTHERN RAILWAY COMPANY, Defendant, and The Wisconsin Central Railroad Company, Charles L. Colby, Edwin H. Abbot, and John A. Stewart & Edwin H. Abbot as Trustees, Garnishees. } At Law.

This day came the defendant, The Milwaukee & Northern Railway Company, by its counsel, Mr. Mariner, and moved the court for leave to amend its answer as follows:

Motion of Mil. & N. R'y Co. to Amend its Answer.

Circuit Court of the United States, Eastern District of Wisconsin.

THE BROOKS LOCOMOTIVE WORKS
vs.
THE MILWAUKEE & NORTHERN RAILWAY COMPANY, EDWIN H. ABBOTT, JOHN A. STEWART, *et al.*, Garnishees.

And now comes the said defendant, by E. Mariner, its attorney, and prays leave to amend its answer in this cause by inserting the words "from and after the first day of May, 1879," after the words "as aforesaid were", in the second line of the second paragraph of said answer,

37

E. MARINER,
Att'y for the Deft, The Milwaukee & Northern R'y Co.

Order Overruling Motion to Amend Answer of Mil. & Northern R'y Co.

And said motion being argued by the counsel of the parties, on consideration thereof it is ordered by the court that said motion be, and hereby is, overruled.

Findings.

And the issues in this cause came on to be tried at the present term of this court, and were tried by the court (a trial by jury having been waived by the written stipulation of the parties filed herein), the Hon. John M. Harlan, associate justice of the Supreme Court of the United States, and the Honorable Charles E. Dyer, district judge of the United States for the eastern district of Wisconsin, presiding, the plaintiff appearing by Messrs. Davis, Riess & Shepard, its attorneys, with Messrs. D. S. Wegg & J. G. Jenkins, of counsel; the defendant, The Milwaukee & Northern Railway Company, by E. Mariner, Esq., its attorney and counsel, and the defendants, Stewart and Abbot, by Finches, Lynde & Miller, their attorneys and counsel; and the said court, having heard the allegations and proofs of the parties, does hereby find and determine thereupon the following 38 facts to be established by the evidence and the following conclusions of law thereupon:

Facts.

First. That on the 30th day of November, 1875, the plaintiff above named duly recovered a judgment in this court against The Milwaukee & Northern Railway Company, defendant herein, for the sum of $15,368.72, damages and costs; that said judgment is still in full force and wholly unpaid and unsatisfied; that there is now due thereon from said defendant, The Milwaukee and Northern Railway Company, to said plaintiff the said sum of $15,368.72, with interest at the rate of seven per cent. per annum from the 30th day of November, 1875, amounting at this date to the sum of $23,410.40, and that said judgment was rendered upon certain promissory notes given by said company to the plaintiff upon the sale of an engine furnished for its railroad on the 6th day of September, 1873; that an *alias* execution was duly issued out of and under the seal of this court to the marshal of the eastern district of Wisconsin upon said judgment on the 7th day of July, 1879, and while the same was in the hands of the said marshal, and wholly unsatisfied, and before the return day thereof, to wit, on the 7th day of July, 1879, 39 this action was commenced, by due service of the garnishee affidavit and summons herein, upon the said defendant and upon the garnishees named in the title of this cause.

Second. That the Wisconsin Central Railroad Company was, at said last-named date, and for many years prior thereto had been, and at all times hereinafter mentioned was, a corporation created by and under the laws of the State of Wisconsin, and owned and operated a railroad from Menasha, in the State of Wisconsin, to Ashland, on Lake Superior, in said State; that the defendant, The Milwaukee & Northern Railway Company, was during said times a corporation created by and under the laws of the State of Wisconsin, and owned a certain main line of railway extending from the city of Milwaukee, in the State of Wisconsin, to the city of Green Bay, in said State, and a spur line from Hilbert Junction, on said main line, to Menasha aforesaid; that the said Wisconsin Central Railroad Company, on the first day of July, 1871, mortgaged its line of railway aforesaid to secure certain bonds therein mentioned, which mortgage was in the usual form of railway mortgages, and 40 authorized the trustees, upon default, to take possession of said railway, and that at all times hereinafter mentioned the defendants, John A. Stewart and Edwin H. Abbot, were the trustees under said mortgage.

Third. That the Milwaukee & Northern Railway Company, prior to the times hereinafter mentioned, had duly mortgaged its said line of railway to secure its bonds, in the usual form of railway mortgages, with authority upon the part of the trustees in said mortgage named to take possession of said railway upon default in the payment of the principal or interest of the bonds thereby secured, and that at the times hereinafter mentioned Jesse Hoyt and A. Warren Greenleaf were the trustees in said mortgage named, a copy of which mortgage is hereto annexed, marked "Exhibit A."

Fourth. That on the 9th day of November, 1873, the Milwaukee and Northern Railway Company leased to the Wisconsin Central Railroad Company its line of railway and appurtenances, motive power and rolling-stock, railroad materials, and supplies of every, description for the term of 999 years from and after November 30th' 1873, a copy of which case is hereto annexed, marked Exhibit "B;'

41   that by supplemental agreements to said lease, of which "Exhibits C. & D," hereto annexed, are copies, Jesse Hoyt was substituted as trustee in the place of the Wisconsin Marine & Fire Insurance Company Bank, and that said lease was on or about January 8th, 1878, by said Milwaukee & Northern Railway Company assigned to Jesse Hoyt and A. Warren Greenleaf, trustees under said mortgage, of which the Wisconsin Central Railway Company had notice, copies of which assignment and notice are hereto annexed, marked "Exhibits E & F;" that the Wisconsin Central Railway Company entered into possession of said road under said lease and continued therein until the garnishees herein, Stewart and Abbot, took possession of said railway in January, 1879, and said company paid rent under said lease.

Fifth. That at the times herein mentioned Jesse Hoyt was the president of the Milwaukee & Northern Railway Company, and Angus Smith was the vice-president thereof.

Sixth. That on the 9th day of January, 1875, a foreclosure of the mortgage made by the Milwaukee & Northern Railway Company was commenced in this court by Jesse Hoyt, surviving trustee, against

42   The Milwaukee & Northern Railway Company and The Wisconsin Central Railway Company, defendants, but that no receiver was appointed therein until the 28th day of April, 1879, on which day the said court, by consent of the parties to said suit, made an order annulling such case and appointing James C. Spencer receiver, who qualified as such receiver on the 5th day of May, 1879, a copy of which order is hereto annexed, marked "Exhibit G," and that said trustees had never taken posession of said railroad and property under said mortgage, nor claimed so to do, until the appointment of said receiver.

Seventh. That on the 12th day of October, 1875, one James Ludington recovered a judgment at law, in the circuit court of the State of Wisconsin for the county of Milwaukee, against The Milwaukee & Northern Railway Company, and on the 15th day of November, 1875, caused an execution to be issued thereon, which was returned *nulla bona* on the 18th day of January, 1876, which judgment was rendered upon default and without any appearance by the defendant therein, and the process commencing said action was served only upon Guido Pfister, a director of said company, and upon no other officer or person.

Eighth. That on the 17th day of November, 1875, the said
43   James Ludington filed a bill in equity in said circuit court
for the county of Milwaukee founded upon his said judgment at law, and on the 27th day of December, 1875, obtained a decree therein directing the sale of the railroad of The Milwaukee & Northern Railway Company thereunder; that on the 4th day of March, 1876, under said decree, the sheriff of the county of Milwaukee sold said railroad to Guido Pfister, and on the 29th day of March, 1876, executed a deed thereof to him, but did not make a report of the sale to the court until January 30th, 1880, and said sale was confirmed by the court on the 9th day of February, 1880, and that the sheriff's deed to Guido Pfister was recorded in the office of the register of deeds of the county of Milwaukee on the 26th day of February, 1880, but said Pfister never took or claimed possession under said deed.

Ninth. On the 4th day of January, 1879, the defendants, John A. Stewart and Edwin H. Abbot, as trustees under the mortgage of the Wisconsin Central Railroad Company, said company having theretofore made default under said mortgage, and then being so in default, duly
took possession of said Wisconsin Central railroad under the
44   said mortgage, and also took possession of the Milwaukee &
Northern railway, and thereupon notified the Milwaukee & Northern Railway Company and Jesse Hoyt, trustee of the mortgage of said company, and trustee under its said lease to the Wisconsin Central Railroad Company, and as assignee of said lease, of the taking of such possession of the Milwaukee and Northern railway, and notifying that they declined to assume, affirm, or in any way ratify the lease thereof to the Wisconsin Central Railroad Company, and notifying that, unless said parties notified should otherwise elect, they would continue to operate said Milwaukee & Northern railway temporarily and for such compensation as that service might fairly be worth, and requesting a personal interview to ascertain their wishes and with a view to a more permanent arrangement, and offering to submit to the parties in interest any proposition which could be jointly recommended with reference to the future possession of said railway, of which notice "Exhibit H," hereto annexed, is a copy; that the said Milwaukee & Northern Railway Company, or Jesse Hoyt as president or as trustee, or as assignee of said lease, did not, nor did either of them, in any way object to the possession of said
45   railroad by said Stewart and Abbot, or give any attention to
said notice until the commencement of negotiations in March, 1879, but said Stewart and Abbot continued to use and operate the Milwaukee & Northern railway without further arrangement or agreement, and without any objection by any of the parties to this proceeding, and with the acquiescence of the Wisconsin Central Railroad Company, but without any assignment of the lease, until

the 1st day of May,. 1879, and until the lease from the receiver as hereinafter found; and said Milwaukee and Northern Railway Company and said Jesse Hoyt, shortly before the 1st day of May, 1879, in the presence and with the concurrence of all others interested, including the Wisconsin Central Railway Company, had negotiations with them which culminated in an arrangement by which a receiver of the Milwaukee & Northern railway was appointed in the foreclosure suit, as hereinbefore found; that said Stewart and Abbot then entered into a lease with said receiver of said Milwaukee & Northern railway for a certain term commencing on the 1st day of May, 1879; that on or about

46

the 23rd day of July, 1879, after the service of the garnishee affidavit and summons herein, it was arranged and agreed between said Stewart and Abbot, trustees, on the one part, and Josse Hoyt as trustee and assignee, upon the other part, that the sum of $28,258.44 was the amount properly payable by the said Stewart and Abbot as trustees to the party lawfully entitled to receive the same out of the moneys received by said trustees from the operation of the Milwaukee & Northern railway from January 3rd, 1879, to May 1st, 1879, and for the use thereof, which amount was a less sum than would have been coming by the terms of the lease to the Wisconsin Central railroad, and that thereupon said Stewart and Abbot paid to said Jesse Hoyt as such trustee and assignee the said sum of money upon receiving a bond of indemnity executed by Ephraim Mariner, Guido Pfister, and Angus Smith indemnifying them against this suit by reason of such payment, copies of which agreement of accounting and bond of indemnity are hereto annexed, marked "Exhibits I & J."

Tenth. That on the 8th day of March, 1880, an order was made in the foreclosure suit of the mortgage of the Milwaukee & Northern

47

Railway Company for the sale of said railroad, which sale took place on the 5th day of June, 1880, and was sold to Ephraim Mariner and Guido Pfister as trustees for the holders of the bonds under said mortgage; that on the 9th day of June the report of said sale was filed, and was confirmed by the court, and that thereafter, on the 3rd day of July, 1880, the final report of the receiver was filed, asking for a discharge, and said report was confirmed on the 5th day of July, 1879.

Eleventh. That from January 3rd, 1879, to May 1st, 1879, the said Stewart and Abbot were not in possession of or operating said Milwaukee & Northern railway under any lease whatever between them and James C. Spencer as receiver of the Milwaukee & Northern railway, as claimed in the answer of the principal defendant herein, nor was the indebtedness of said garnishees for the use and occupation of said railroad during said period owing by them to said James C. Spencer, receiver.

Conclusions of Law.

The contention in this case being as to who was entitled to the sum of $28,258.44, agreed upon as the fair compensation for the use of the Milwaukee & Northern railway from January 3rd to May 1st, 1879, we find:

48   First. That it did not belong to and cannot be rightfully claimed by the receiver appointed in the foreclosure suit of the mortgage on the Milwaukee & Northern railway for the reason that he was not qualified as receiver until a subsequent date, and had never reduced the property to possession, and was only receiver of the mortgaged property.

Second. That said fund did not belong to the Wisconsin Central Railroad Company, because such occupation and operation of the road by Stewart and Abbot, trustees, were with its acquiescence, and, it is upon record in this cause as denying all indebtedness to the principal defendant herein, and makes no claim to said fund.

Third. That said fund did not belong to Jesse Hoyt as trustee under said mortgage, because said trustee had not taken possession of said railroad, and was not entitled to the income thereof; that it did not belong to said Jesse Hoyt as trustee under said case or as assignee of said case, because the occupation and operation of said road by Stewart and Abbot, trustees, was not under said case, but in defiance thereof and in opposition thereto.

Fourth. That said sum was, at the time of the garnishee 49   proceedings herein, the property of the Milwaukee and Northern Railway Company, and was liable to be taken and attached for the debts due by said company; that the plaintiff, by virtue of the garnishee proceedings herein upon Stewart and Abbot, trustees, acquired a lawful claim and lien upon said fund to the extent of the plaintiff's judgment and debt against said company, and that at the time of said garnishment the said John A. Stewart and Edwin H. Abbot had in their hands belonging to the defendant, The Milwaukee and Northern Railway Company, and were indebted to and owed said company for the use and occupation by said Stewart and Abbot of the railway of said company from January 3rd to May 1st, 1879, the sum of $28,258.44, and that the plaintiff is entitled to judgment against said Stewart and Abbot for the said amount due upon its judgment, to wit, the sum of $23,410.40; that as to the garnishees, The Wisconsin Central Railroad Company and Charles L. Colby, this action should be dismissed.

Let judgment be entered herein in favor of the plaintiff against John A. Stewart and Edwin H. Abbot for the sum of $23,410.40, with costs to be taxed.

Dated May 21st, 1883.

                    JOHN M. HARLAN,
                        Circuit Justice.
                CHAS. E. DYER,
                        Dist. Judge.

50   EXHIBIT "A."

This indenture, made the first day of December, in the year of our Lord one thousand eight hundred and seventy, by and between The Milwaukee and Northern Railway Company, a corporation duly incorporated and organized under and pursuant to an act of the

Legislature of the State of Wisconsin, entitled "An act to incorporate The Milwaukee and Northern Railway Company," approved February 24th, 1870, and located in said State, party of the first part, and Jesse Hoyt and A. Warren Greenleaf, of the city of New York, as trustees, parties of the second part—

Whereas The Milwaukee and Northern Railway Company is now engaged in constructing the first division, so called, of its railway, being that part extending from the city of Milwaukee to the city of Green Bay, in said State, together with all branches that are authorized by law, from points on the last-named part of the trunk road to Lake Michigan, Lake Winnebago, or Fox river; and

Whereas the said company, party of the first part hereto, has, by resolution of its board of directors (which, under its said act of incorporation, has control and management of its corporate affairs), determined to borrow money on an issue of bonds not to exceed three million five hundred thousand dollars in their aggregate principal amount, nor to exceed four thousand bonds in number, one thousand of which bonds are to be for the principal sum of five hundred dollars each, and the remaining three thousand of which

51   are to be for the principal sum of one thousand dollars each, all to bear interest at the rate of eight per centum per annum, interest payable in semi-annual installments, on the first day of June and of December in each and every year, in the city of New York, free from all United States Government tax, and all of which bonds are to be equally secured by these presents, and are to be of the following form of bond and coupon in substance, except as to the difference in denomination as aforesaid—that is to say:

No. —. $. —.

The Milwaukee & Northern Railway Company.

UNITED STATES OF AMERICA, *State of Wisconsin:*

First Mortgage Bond.

Principal and interest payable in New York city. Interest at eight per cent., free from U. S. Government tax.

Know all men by these presents that The Milwaukee and Northern Railway Company hereby, for value received, undertakes and promises to pay to Jesse Hoyt and A. Warren Greenleaf, or bearer, twenty years after the date hereof, at said company's office or agency in the city of New York, the sum of one thousand dollars, and interest thereon at the rate of eight per centum per annum, payable in semi-annual installments on the first day of December and of June in each and every year from date till paid, on the presentation and surrender of the annexed coupons as they severally become due, interest to be free from United States Government tax.

This bond is one of a series of four thousand bonds, numbered consecutively from number one to number four thousand, both inclusive, all bearing even date herewith, all of similar tenor herewith, except that one thousand of said bonds, numbered from

number one to number one thousand, both inclusive, are for the principal sum of five hundred dollars each, and the remaining three thousand thereof, numbered from number one thousand and one to number four thousand, both inclusive, are for the princi-
52 pal sum of one thousand dollars each, amounting in the aggregate to three million five hundred thousand dollars, and all equally secured by a first mortgage or deed of trust on the first division, so called, of the said company's railway, being that part of such railway which extends from Milwaukee to Green Bay, and all branches from points on the part of the trunk road last named terminating on Lake Michigan, Lake Winnebago, or Fox river, its furniture, equipments, and appurtenances, and all of said company's corporate franchises and rights pertaining to said first division, executed and given to Jesse Hoyt and A. Warren Green-leaf, of the city of New York, trustees, in trust for the benefit and security of the holders of the said series of bonds of which this is one, or of such and so many thereof as shall be issued and sold, and containing power and authority to the said trustees to take posses-sion of said railway, equipments, property, appurtenances, and fran-chises, and to use or sell the same in case of default for the space of six months in payment of interest on any of said bonds, or of any taxes or assessments due on said property, or any part thereof, in case of which default it is therein provided that the whole principal sum of such of said bonds as are then outstanding and unpaid shall also become due and payable at once, as though the same had been made originally payable at that time.

The said bonds are to be issued from time to time, as the con-struction progresses, at the rate of $14,000 for every mile of said rail-way which shall be completed by the laying of the iron rails ready for use, and $4,000 additional (making $18,000 in the whole) for each and every mile so finished, and also supplied with convenient rolling-stock and furniture ready for actual operation, and not faster. Within the limitation last named the company will issue bonds of either or both denominations aforesaid at its discretion.

The said mortgage or deed of trust has been duly executed, acknowledged, and recorded in the office of the secretary of state of the State of Wisconsin, pursuant to statute in such case made and provided, and each bond is, or is to be stamped before its
53 issue, in compliance with the internal revenue laws of the United States.

This bond shall pass by delivery, except when by registration and endorsement, as hereinafter provided, it shall be rendered transfer-able only on the books of the company, in which latter-named case it shall pass by transfer on the books of the company in the city of New York, or in any other place which may be designated by the company for that purpose.

After the registration of ownership, certified by endorsement hereon by the transfer agent of the company, no transfer except upon the books of the company shall be valid, unless the last trans-fer be to bearer, which shall restore the quality of transferability by delivery, but this bond shall continue subject to successive registrations and transfers to bearer as aforesaid at the option of each holder. On a registration of ownership the holder may at his option surrender the coupons, which shall then be cancelled, and thereafter interest will be payable only to the registered holder or his attorney.

In witness whereof the said company has caused its corporate seal to be hereunto affixed and these presents to be signed by its president and attested by its secretary this first day of December, in the year of our Lord eighteen hundred and seventy.

O. H. WALDO,
President of the Milwaukee & Northern Railway Company.

Attest: WM. TAINTOR, *Secretary.*

The Milwaukee & Northern Railway Company will pay to bearer at said company's agency in the city of New York, on the first day of —, A. D. 18—, forty dollars, for six months' interest on the bond of said company for $1,000. Dated Dec. 1st, 1870. No. —.

WM. TAINTOR, *Secretary.*

Now, therefore, this indenture witnesseth that the said party of the first part, for the purpose of securing and rendering more sure the payment of the principal sums of money mentioned and provided for in said bonds bearing even date herewith, and in each and every of them, with interest thereon, accruing after actual issue, according to the true intent and meaning thereof, and in consideration of the premises, of the loan of said money, and of the sum of one dollar to the party of the first part in hand paid by the said parties of the second part at and before the ensealing and delivery of these presents, the receipt whereof is hereby confessed by the said party of the first part, the Milwaukee and Northern Railway Company, the party of the first part aforesaid, hath granted, bargained, sold, assigned, transferred, and conveyed, and by these presents doth grant, bargain, sell, assign, transfer, and convey, to the said Jesse Hoyt and A. Warren Greenleaf as trustees, the parties of the second part aforesaid, and to the survivors of them, and to their successor and successors in such trust, and to their assigns in fee forever, the whole of the said first division of the railway of the said party of the first part, embracing all that part of their trunk railway, constructed and to be constructed, extending from the city of Milwaukee to the city of Green Bay, in the State of Wisconsin, and any and all branches, constructed and to be constructed, from any point or points on said part of said trunk railway to any point or points on either Lake Michigan, Lake Winnebago, or Fox river, with all fixtures and appurtenances thereto, together with all and singular the lands, depot grounds, ways, rights of way, buildings, viaducts, culverts, bridges, and rails, and all erections and superstructure of every kind, all tools, implements, furniture, rolling-stock, materials, and movable property of every kind (all the chattels and movable property hereinbefore mentioned and embraced being hereby declared and agreed to be fixtures and appurtenances of said first division of said railway, and to be used and sold therewith, if at all, and not separately therefrom, and to be regarded and treated as part thereof), and together with all improvements and additions made and to be made to any or all of the said railways or railroads, properties, and appurtenances by said party of the first part, 55 or by others; also all easements, leasehold estates, terms of years and parts of terms, all rights and underleases, agreements, covenants, and contracts of any and every kind connected with, relating to, or made in any manner for the convenience of the said first division of said railway or its business; also all bills, incomes, issues, earnings, and profits of or arising from the said first division, and all corporate rights, privileges, liberties, and franchises of the said party of the first part in any way pertaining to said first division, or any part thereof, or to the acquisition, construction, maintenance, use, employment, and operation thereof, and also all and every other estate, interest, property, or thing, right, privilege, or franchise which said party of the first part now owns or holds, or shall hereafter acquire or hold, necessary or convenient for the use, occupation, operation, and enjoyment of all or any of its said railways, leases and property, privileges and franchises, or any part or portion thereof; but nothing herein contained shall be held or construed to prevent said party of the first part (by and with the consent in writing of said parties of the second part, or their successors in said trust) from selling, hypothecating, or otherwise disposing of any lands or other property and effects, real or personal, not essential or necessary to be retained for the convenient use of the said railways, nor from selling shares, nor from collecting and using about its business money due on its capital stock, subscriptions, or otherwise, provided that said party of the first part shall diligently proceed to apply all such means and proceeds to the construction, completing, repairing, and equipping of its said railways, and to other like necessary purposes thereof, nor from receiving and using in and about its proper business the income and earnings of its said railways, and provided also that no default shall have been made and at the time exist in the payment of the interest or principal of any of the bonds hereby secured. Either before or after default in payment of interest the trustees, for the time being, of said trusts shall have full power in their discretion, upon the written request of the said party of the first part, to convey, by way of release or otherwise, to persons designated by said party of the first part, 56 any lands acquired or held by said company for the purpose of its track, buildings, works, fixtures, and appurtenances, and which, in the judgment of said trustees, shall not be necessary for use in connection with said railway or railways; also any land once used by the company, but which may become disused by reason of the change of location of any part of the said company's track, buildings, works, fixtures, and appurtenances, and all such lands, however occupied, as said party of the first part may deem it expedient to disuse or abandon by reason of such change; also to consent to any change that may be deemed expedient in the location of any part of the said company's tracks, buildings, works, fixtures, and appurtenances, and to make and deliver all conveyances and contracts necessary to carry the same into effect. But any and all

lands which may be acquired for permanent use in substitution for any property so released shall be conveyed to the trustees upon the trusts herein created and declared, and said trustees shall also have power to allow the said party of the first part, from time to time, to dispose of such portions of the equipment, machinery, implements, and personal property upon or connected and used with said first division, or at any time acquired or held for the use thereof, as may have become unfit for such use, replacing the same by new and suitable articles, which shall at once become subject to the operation of these presents and the uses and trusts hereby created as fully as if the same were now the property of said party of the first part, and were now affixed to and a part of said first division of the said railway: To have and to hold the estate, property, rights, privileges, franchises, and interests of the said party of the first part, together with all and singular the emoluments, income, and advantages, tenements, hereditaments, and appurtenances thereunto belonging or in anywise appertaining, and the reversion and reversions, remainder or remainders, rents, issues, and profits thereof, unto the said Jesse Hoyt and A. Warren Greenleaf, parties of the second part, their survivor and their successor and successors in the trusts hereby created, and assigns forever, on the trusts and for the uses and purposes herein declared, and no other: Provided always, That
57   these presents are made upon the express condition that if the said party of the first part shall well and truly pay or cause to be paid to the holders of said bonds or obligations intended to be hereby secured, and each and every of them after the same shall be issued, the principal sums of money therein respectively mentioned, at the maturity thereof, according to their true intent and meaning, with the interest thereon accruing at the times and in the way and manner therein provided, according to the true intent and meaning of these presents, that then and from thenceforth this indenture and the estate hereby granted shall cease, determine, and be utterly void and of no effect, without any release or formal reconveyance, reentry, acknowledgment of satisfaction, or any other act whatsoever, but, nevertheless, upon such full payment and satisfaction being made, it shall be the duty of said trustees, or their survivor or the successor or successors of them in said trust, to make, execute, and deliver to said party of the first part a formal release and discharge of this mortgage in due and legal form, properly executed and acknowledged, so as to be entitled to record under the laws of said State.

And the said party of the first part, in consideration of the premises, hereby covenants and agrees to and with the said Jesse Hoyt and A. Warren Greenleaf, their survivor or sucessors or successor in said trust, and assigns, that the said party of the first part will at any time or times hereafter, upon the reasonable request of said parties of the second|part, their survivor, successors, or successor in this trust, or assigns, execute and deliver, or cause to be executed and delivered, all and every such further and reasonable deeds, conveyances, assignments, and assurances in the law for the better and more effectual vesting and confirming the premises hereby granted, or intended so to be, and especially for conveying any property, interests, rights, privileges, powers, or franchises subsequently to the date hereof acquired by the said party of the first part, and comprehended or intended to be comprehended in the description contained in these presents, if any such there be, which shall not inure, by virtue hereof, to

58 the use and benefit of the holders of said bonds, to the said parties of the second part, their survivor, successors or successor, and assigns, as by them or their counsel, learned in the law, shall be reasonably devised, advised, or required for the better effectuating of these presents; and further that the said party of the first part the above-bargained premises, property, and franchises in the quiet and peaceful possession of the said parties of the second part and their survivor and successors or successor and assigns, against all and every person or persons lawfully claiming the whole or any part thereof, will forever warrant and defend; and further that the said party of the first part will do and perform all things on the part of the said party of the first part to be done and performed as hereinbefore set forth, and will faithfully apply all the money and other things arising from the issue of said bonds in good faith to the construction of said railroad and branches, and to putting the same into operation, and to the purposes hereinbefore recited and mentioned as the objects thereof until the same are fully accomplished.

And further that said party of the first part will pay to the several holders of the said bonds, respectively, the said principal sums of money therein respectively mentioned, and, as expressed therein, and the interest thereon as the same shall become due and payable, and will pay all taxes and assessments of every name and nature upon the said property, or upon the earnings or income thereof, when the same are due, and before any costs or expenses shall have been caused by the non-payment thereof; and further, in case of default in the payment of any part of said interest on any day when the same becomes due and payable, and of such default continuing for a period of six months, that then the whole amount of said principal sum of such of said bonds as are then outstanding, and interest thereon to that time, shall, at the option of said parties of the second part, their survivor or successors or successor in said trust, be deemed to become, and shall be, due and payable at once, and the said party of the first part shall and will, on demand made by said parties of the second part, their survivor or their successors

59 or successor or assigns, trustee, or trustees for the time being, or their agent or agents, duly authorized in writing, assign and transfer, in due form, to them or their agent or agents so authorized the actual possession of all the herein granted and conveyed property and premises, rights, and franchises herein recited and mentioned or intended to be embraced in this trust.

And further that the expense of taking, holding, and managing said premises and property if possession be taken shall be paid from the income, and if necessary from the avails of the sales of said premises, property, and franchises by such trustee or trustees as aforesaid, as the same may be for the time being; and further that

5—226

in such case the said parties of the second part, their survivor or
successors or successor in said trust and assigns, shall and may themselves, or by their agents and officers, take and receive, collect, and
have the income and profits of said railways and property, first ap-
plying the same to the payment and discharge of all current necessary expenses of operating and repairs, including the expenses
hereinbefore mentioned, and all taxes and other similar charges on
said property or its earnings, and next to the payment of all sums
of money due and payable upon the aforesaid bonds issued by said
party of the first part, and hereby secured according to the tenor
thereof; and further that the said parties of the second part, their
survivor or their successors or successor in said trust or assigns, the
said default still continuing, and having continued for six months,
at his or their discretion, and with the approbation or at the request
of the holders of at least twenty per centum of the bonds hereby
secured and then outstanding unpaid, shall proceed to sell and
dispose of, or cause to be sold and disposed of, all the estate
premises, property, rights, franchises, and interests hereby conveyed or intended to be conveyed, or so much thereof as shall be
necessary to pay and discharge the principal and interest according to the tenor thereof of all such of said bonds hereby secured
and then outstanding as may have been issued by the said party
of the first part, and which shall then remain unpaid, and all the
expenses herein contemplated and authorized, together with all
benefit and equity of redemption of said party of the first
60   part therein, at public auction, in the city of Milwaukee, to
the highest bidder, having previously given public notice of
the time, place, and terms of said sale, and of the specific property to be
sold, by publishing the same in at least two newspapers of good cir-
culation in the last-named city, and wherever else the trustees may
deem expedient or the law may require, for a period of at least three
months previous to such sale, and for such further period, if any, that
the law may require and as the attorney or attorneys of said
party of the first part for that purpose, by these presents duly constituted and appointed, make, execute, and deliver to the purchaser
or purchasers thereof a good and sufficient deed or deeds of conveyance in the law for the same, granting and assuring to said purchaser or purchasers all such estate, right, property, and interest,
and to the same extent as the said party of the first part hath therein
at the date of these presents, or shall have at any time subsequently
thereto, and also a good and sufficient assignment of said personal
property, choses in action, contracts, and leases, and out of the
moneys arising from the sale or sales to retain the cost and charges
of advertisement of the said sale of the premises, and all other sum
and sums of money which said trustees, their survivor or the successors or successor of them in said trust, may have been obliged to
pay by reason of their taking upon themselves and executing said
trusts, including the expense of taking possession of and operating
said premises, and a reasonable amount for their own services and
for legal professional advice, aid, and assistance in effecting and con-
summating said possession, operation, and sale, and in the perform-

ance of all their duties in and about or growing out of said trust, or the execution thereof, and also the principal and interest which shall then remain due and unpaid on said bonds remaining issued and outstanding, and hereby secured as aforesaid, for the benefit of and to be paid to the holders thereof, and then to restore the residue and remainder of the proceeds of sale, if any, to the said party of the first part, it being hereby expressly understood and agreed that the bonds issued by said party of the first part, and secured 61 by these presents, shall be ratably received in payment of said sale by said trustees, or the survivor or the successors or successor of them, in case any such sale shall be made, at the option of the holder or holders thereof, and such sale, when fully consummated, shall be a perpetual bar, both in law and in equity, against the said party of the first part and persons claiming or to claim the premises, or any part thereof, or any interest therein, by, through, or under the said party of the first part, subsequent to the date of these presents.

And this indenture further witnesseth, that these presents and the said bonds hereby secured, or intended to be, are made, executed, and issued or delivered upon the terms, conditions, and agreements following—that is to say:

First. That the actual possession, use, management, and control of all the hereinbefore-granted estate, premises, property, rights, franchises, and interests shall be and remain in and with the said party of the first part so long as the bonds hereby secured shall be or remain without default.

Second. That the said bonds shall be countersigned or certified by the said parties of the second part, and shall be issued and put out only to such an amount as shall be at and after the rate of fourteen thousand dollars in bonds per mile in length of the track of so much of said railway and branches as is completed by laying of the iron rails ready for use, and four thousand dollars additional, making eighteen thousand dollars in the aggregate per mile of such completed road when supplied with convenient rolling-stock and furniture ready for actual operation.

Third. That in case of any vacancy in the said trusteeship by the death, resignation, incapacity to act by sickness, absence from the United States permanently or for more than six months, or from any other cause, of either of the trustees, all his estate, right, interest, power, and control shall be thereupon divested and cease and determine, but without destroying and without discontinuing or vacating the trust, and the said company, party of the first part, and the surviving trustee, party of the second part, shall by deed select and appoint a new trustee to fill the vacancy so occurring, and in case of disagreement between said com-62 pany and such remaining trustee, or of delay on their part for the period of three months after such vacancy occurs, to make such selection and appointment, the supreme court of said State, or a majority of the judges thereof, or the judge of the circuit court for Milwaukee county, upon request of the holders of at least twenty per centum of the amount of said bonds hereby secured and then outstanding, may, by order, appoint a new trustee or trustees to fill such vacancy, and such proceedings may be had and appointments and selections made as often as the like occasion may require the appointment of a trustee to execute the trusts herein declared, and when so selected and appointed such new trustee shall thereupon become vested, for the purpose of the said trust, with all the estate, rights, interests, powers, property, and control hereby conveyed or granted to or vested in the said Jesse Hoyt and A. Warren Greenleaf, parties of the second part, by these presents, without any further or other assurance, grant, or conveyance of the same, as fully and effectually as if such appointment had been originally made herein.

But if the same shall be necessary both the said party of the first part and such new trustee, or either of them, shall make, execute, and deliver all necessary conveyances, agreements, contracts, grants, powers, and authorities for that purpose.

And it is also further understood and agreed by and between the parties to these presents that the said parties of the second part, the survivor or the successors or successor of them in said trusts, shall be accountable for only reasonable diligence in the management thereof, and shall not be responsible for the acts of each other to which they do not severally assent, nor for the acts or negligences of any agent or agents necessarily or properly employed by them when such agent or agents are selected with proper and reasonable discretion, or with the approbation of the said party of the first part, and that the officers of the said railway company shall at all times have the right to inspect the books and all accounts kept by any such trustee, or their agent or agents or receivers, when in possession of said property, or any part thereof; and this indenture hereby
63   further witnesseth that said parties of the second part hereby accept the aforesaid trusts, and also covenant and agree to and with the said party of the first part to execute the same upon the terms and conditions hereinbefore, as well as hereinafter, mentioned and provided, and which said terms and conditions are hereby mutually agreed to and upon by both of the parties to these presents.

In testimony whereof the said party of the first part, in pursuance of authority given by law and by resolution of its board of directors, hath caused these presents to be sealed with its corporate seal and to be signed by O. H. Waldo, its president, and William Taintor, its secretary, and the said parties of the second part have hereunto subscribed their names and affixed their seals the day and year first above written. It is understood that each of the bonds to be secured by these presents shall, when certified and issued, be duly stamped under and according to the revenue laws of the United States.

                    THE MILWAUKEE AND NORTHERN
                        RAILWAY COMPANY,
[SEAL.]   By O. H. WALDO, *President.*
                    WM. TAINTOR, *Secretary.*

Signed, sealed, and delivered by The Milwaukee and Northern Railway Company, by its president and secretary, in presence of—

FRANK B. VAN VALKENBURGH.

ROBERT V. V. WALDO.

JESSE HOYT. [SEAL.]

A. W. GREENLEAF. [SEAL.]

Signed, sealed, and delivered by Jesse Hoyt and A. Warren Greenleaf, as trustees, in presence of—

J. A. ELLIS.

THOS. SADLER.

64 STATE OF WISCONSIN, }
     County of Milwaukee, } ss :

Be it remembered that on this second day of December, in the year of our Lord one thousand eight hundred and seventy, before me, a notary public for the State of Wisconsin, duly commissioned and residing in said county of Milwaukee, and duly authorized to administer oaths and take acknowledgments of deeds, personally came Otis H. Waldo, the president, and William Taintor, the secretary, of the Milwaukee and Northern Railway Company of the State of Wisconsin, each of whom is to me personally known, and each of whom, being by me severally and duly sworn, doth severally say on oath that the said Otis H. Waldo is the president of said company, and that the said William Taintor is the secretary of said company; that he knows the corporate seal of said company; that the seal affixed to the foregoing instrument is such corporate seal of said company; that said seal was thereto affixed by order of the board of directors of said company; that the said Otis H. Waldo signed his name thereto as president, and said William Taintor signed his name thereto as secretary, by the like order of said board of directors, and they thereupon also severally acknowledged the execution of said foregoing deed as the free act and deed of said company, the party of the first part mentioned herein, for the uses and purposes therein mentioned.

In witness whereof I have hereunto set my hand and affixed my official seal, at Milwaukee, the day and year above written.

[SEAL.]   FRANK B. VAN VALKENBURG,

Notary Public, Residing in the City and County of

Milwaukee, State of Wisconsin.

STATE OF NEW YORK, }
City and County of New York, } ss :

Be it remembered that on the ninth day of December, A. D. 1870, before me, Thomas Sadler, a commissioner in and for the State 65 of New York, duly appointed and commissioned by the Governor of the State of Wisconsin to take the acknowledgment and proof of deeds and other instruments of writing, to be used or recorded in said State of Wisconsin, personally came Jesse Hoyt and A. W. Greenleaf, to me personally known, and known to be the persons who executed the foregoing deed of trust or mortgage, and each for himself acknowledged; that he executed the same freely and voluntarily, for the purposes therein mentioned.

Given under my hand and official seal the day and year above written.

[SEAL.]   THOMAS SADLER,
                    Commissioner of Wisconsin, 11 *Wall Street, N. Y.*

66   EXHIBIT " B."

This indenture of lease made this eighth day of November, A. D. 1873, by and between the Milwaukee and Northern Railway Company, party of the first part, and the Wisconsin Central Railroad Company, party of the second part, witnesseth:

That the first party, in consideration of the agreements of the second party hereinafter contained, has let, demised, and leased, and by these presents does let, demise, and lease, unto the second party all that part of the railroad constructed by the first party extending from its terminus in Milwaukee county to Green Bay, together with the branch to Menasha, all in the State of Wisconsin, and all its tracks, depots, and depot grounds, rights of way, bridges, side tracks, turn-tables, water tanks, engine-houses, shops, and buildings, and all its motive power and rolling-stock of every description, its iron rails, fish-plates, spikes, tools, implements, railroad materials, and supplies of every description now on hand for the construction and repair of said railroad, and all its property of every sort and description, rights, liberties, franchises, and privileges belonging to said first party in any way appertaining to the demised premises, subject to a certain mortgage executed by the first party to Jesse Hoyt and A. Warren Greenleaf, trustees, to secure payment of its first-mortgage bonds, which are issued or to be issued at the rate of eighteen thousand dollars per mile and no more on said road,
67   dated December 1st, A. D. 1870, and recorded in the office of
          the secretary of state of the State of Wisconsin. A schedule of the demised property is hereto annexed and marked A.

To have and to hold the same for and during the term of nine hundred and ninety-nine years from and after the thirtieth day of November, A. D. eighteen hundred and seventy-three, in undisturbed possession, use, and control unto the second party, its successors and assigns, provided the agreements, covenants, and stipulations made herein by the second party are faithfully performed, and until breach, if any, thereof by the second party its successors or assigns.

Yielding and paying rent therefor as follows, to wit: In and for each year of said term wherein the gross earnings received from the demised premises as hereinafter set forth shall exceed the sum of one million dollars, thirty per cent. of said gross earnings, and in and for each year of said term wherein said gross earnings shall exceed eight hundred thousand dollars, but not exceed one million dollars, thirty-three per centum of said gross earnings, and in and for each year of said term wherein said gross earnings shall be less than eight hundred thousand dollars, thirty-five per cent. of said gross earnings. Upon the first day of February, A. D. eighteen hundred and seventy-four, the second party shall state to the first party an account, as nearly exact as is practicable, of the gross earnings received from and upon the demised premises during the month of December, A. D. eighteen hundred and seventy-three, and shall, semi-annually, state an exact account of said gross earnings for the six months ending May thirty-first and November thirtieth, as soon thereafter as the same can be made up, and within ten months thereafter in any event. Like accounts, approximately made, shall be stated to the first party on the first day of every month of and for the business of the month next but one preceding; and upon said first day of February and the first day of each following month during said term the second party shall pay the amount of rent so approximated, at the rate of thirty-five per cent., until facts show that the earnings will warrant

68   a lower rate, for the month next but one preceding, to such trustee as shall be from time to time jointly selected by the parties hereto upon the trust to keep the same until the next installment of interest is due upon the bonds issued by the first party under their first mortgage, and then to apply the same, or so much thereof as shall be necessary, to the payment of said interest when and as payable, and, if any surplus remain after payment of said interest, to pay the same to the first party, its successors and assigns, unless said surplus or some part thereof is due to the second party for advances, as is hereinafter provided, made to or for the benefit of the first party to pay said interest, and if said surplus, or any part thereof, is so due, then to second party, as hereinafter provided, so much as is due for said advances and interest. But said rent shall not be paid over to the first party until and unless all matured interest has been paid on said bonds and all advances made by the second party on said interest account repaid to said second party, but in every case so much thereof as shall be necessary for that purpose shall be applied, first, to said matured interest, and, second, to the reimbursement of said advances and interest thereon, and the remainder paid over to the first party. All accounts shall be exactly balanced upon the semi-annual statements aforesaid. Until otherwise jointly agreed the Wisconsin Marine and Fire Insurance Company Bank is appointed trustee aforesaid, and every such trustee shall be required to give security, whenever either party so request in writing, in such manner and amount as the parties hereto may agree upon, or any court having jurisdiction in the premises may determine.

Gross earnings herein shall be taken to mean gross receipts less all taxes; and it is agreed that all taxes shall be deducted from the gross receipts and paid by the second party before computation of rent on gross earnings.

And the parties hereto covenant with each other as follows, to wit:

First. The Milwaukee and Northern Railway Company covenants that it is lawfully empowered to make this lease, and that it will maintain and protect the second party in quiet and peaceable

69   use, possession, and enjoyment of the demised premises, and

will warrant and defend the same to the second party during the term aforesaid, or until possession taken for breach, if any, by the second party of its agreements and covenants.

Second. The first party also covenants that it will complete certain constructions, repairs, and improvements enumerated in schedule marked " B," hereto annexed.

Third. The first party also covenants that it will assign to the second party, or, at its election, carry out in the name of the first party, but for the benefit, at the expense, and under the direction of the second party, all outstanding contracts, undertakings, agreements, and connections with other railroads and individuals, so far as the same are assignable and the second party elects, which the first party has made for the operation and improvement of the demised premises.

Fourth. The first party further covenants that it will pay at their maturity, either by a new issue of bonds not larger in amount, nor at a higher rate of interest, nor at a greater rate per mile, than its present first-mortgage bonds, or in such other manner as it may elect without increasing in any way its indebtedness beyond eighteen thousand dollars per mile upon the demised railroad at eight per centum per annum interest its present first-mortgage bonds, and that it will pay all interest when and as the same is due upon said first-mortgage bonds, and forever hold the second party harmless therefrom, and will not issue any more bonds under its present mortgage beyond the amount of eighteen thousand dollars per mile upon the demised premises, and will not in any way make, create, or suffer any other lien or incumbrance whatever upon said demised premises during the term of this agreement without the consent of the second party.

Fifth. The first party further covenants that it will issue bonds under a new mortgage, or otherwise provide means for laying an additional track whenever the second party shall request, and a commission composed of the presidents of both roads and a third person jointly selected by them shall certify that the business of the road requires a second track for its accommodation, and said bonds shall be negotiated and the proceeds applied under the direction of the second party, and the second party shall, if desired, provide for the payment of interest thereon in the same manner as is provided in this indenture in regard to the first-mortgage bonds now outstanding. The first party also agrees that whenever and if the first party takes possession of the demised premises it will pay the second party the fair value of all buildings and permanent improvements made by the second party upon the demised premises and will allow the second party to remove all its own motive power and rolling-stock.

Sixth. The Wisconsin Central Railroad Company agrees to accept the demise and lease of the demised premises, and to operate the same and maintain in first-class condition the railroad of the first party in connection with and as part of its own road, and to keep the same, including all fixtures, tools, implements, and rolling-stock, in good repair, and do all of its own business which it can control over the road of the first party, and use its best efforts to develop the business of both roads alike and make the road of the first party its trunk line from Milwaukee; but this agreement is not intended to preclude it from extending its own road, by lease or otherwise, to Portage city and to Manitowoc.

Seventh. The second party further agrees to keep full and true books of account, showing the business done upon the demised premises, and will credit the first party with its *pro rata* share of the gross earnings upon said demised premises, to wit, the same proportion thereof which the distance [the] freight and passengers are transported over the road of the first party bears to the whole distance they are transported by the second party, and will allow the president, or other officer of the first party duly authorized for that purpose, at all reasonable times to inspect the said books, and will furnish them with full information to ascertain the gross earnings and the proportion thereof to which the first party is entitled, and will allow them to examine the road and rolling-stock and demised premises, and will keep the same in substantially as good working order and repair as they are in when delivered to the second party.

Eighth. The second party also covenants to pay the rent
71   hereinbefore reserved when and as payable, and also covenants, if the rent paid to the trustees aforesaid in any six months previous to the payment of interest on the said first-mortgage bonds is not enough to pay the whole interest then maturing, to advance so much money as may be necessary to take up the balance of the coupons for interest as they become due and payable, and to take them up; and it is expressly agreed between the parties to these presents that for all sums so advanced the second party shall hold said coupons as a lien, and the same is hereby made and constituted *as* a lien on the rent hereby reserved and on all property hereby demised and leased prior to and superior to all other liens except said mortgage until the same be fully reimbursed with interest at eight per centum per annum out of the said rent or otherwise by the first party. It is also agreed that any surplus of rent which appears upon the semi-annual adjustments of accounts shall be paid to the second party, so far as may be needed to cover any advances and interest thereon made to protect the coupons aforesaid, and that only the residue of said surplus, if any, shall be paid to the first party.

Ninth. It is further jointly agreed that, if the second party fails or neglects for the space of six months after written demand made by the first party to perform any of its covenants and agreements herein contained, then it shall be lawful for the first party, in addition to all other remedies at law or in equity, to enter upon the demised premises and repossess itself of the same; and the second party covenants peaceably to surrender the same upon said entry.

In witness whereof the parties hereto have caused these presents to be signed by Angus Smith, vice-president of the Milwaukee and Northern Railway Company, for and in behalf of said company, and by Gardner Colby, president of the Wisconsin Central Railroad Company, for and in behalf of said company, they being thereunto law-

72   fully authorized so to do, and the seals of said companies to
be hereto affixed, this eighth day of November, A. D. 1873,
in the city of Milwaukee and State of Wisconsin.

(Signed)   THE MILWAUKEE AND NORTHERN
                       RAILWAY COMPANY,
          By ANGUS SMITH, *Vice-President.* [SEAL.]
(Signed)   WISCONSIN CENTRAL R. R. CO.,
          By GARDNER COLBY, *President.* [SEAL.]

In presence of—
     O. H. WALDO.

SCHEDULE B.

As provided for in the lease of the Milwaukee and Northern
Railway Company to the Wisconsin Central Railroad Company,
dated November 8th, A. D. 1873—

The Milwaukee and Northern Railway Company agree to fully
complete the depot at Greenleaf station and the depot at Ledgeville
before the first day of January, A. D. 1874, and to fully complete
the fencing on the whole line of railway to Menasha and Green Bay
on or before the first of July, A. D. 1874.

Agree to connect side track at Lathams with main track on north
end before January 1st, 1874, and to complete the engine-house and
water tank at Green Bay on or before January 1st, 1874.

The said company also agrees to build at Green Bay a depot
similar to that at Depere, and to extend track to north side of block
seven (7) before July 1st, 1874, and to extend tracks in Menasha to
the river above the dam before the close of 1873, and also in the
rear of buildings on the water power before the first of June, 1874,
if the Wisconsin Central Railroad Company so elect.

Agreed to on behalf of the Milwaukee and Northern Railway
Company.

(Signed)   E. B. GREENLEAF,
                                         Gen'l Manager.

Agreed to on behalf of the Wisconsin Central Railroad Company.

73   EXHIBIT "C."

Supplementary agreement made this first day of June, A. D.
   eighteen hundred and seventy-five, by and between the Milwaukee
   and Northern Railway Company and the Wisconsin Central Railroad Company.

Whereas on the eighth day of November, A. D. eighteen hundred
and seventy-three, the Milwaukee and Northern Railway Company,
party of the first part, and the Wisconsin Central Railroad Company, party of the second part, executed a certain indenture of lease
of the Milwaukee and Northern railroad and other property; and
whereas certain modifications of said lease have been mutually by
said companies agreed:

Now, therefore, said companies, for themselves, their successors,
and assigns, respectively do hereby, in addition to the stipulations

of said lease and in modification thereof, so far as those stipulations are inconsistent herewith, agree as follows, to wit:

First. In lieu of the rent reserved in lease and of all advances of money to take up the interest coupons of the Milwaukee and Northern Railway Company, as provided in said lease, the Wisconsin Central Railroad Company shall pay, and the Milwaukee and Northern Railway Company shall accept, for and during the space of three years from and after the first day of June, A. D. eighteen hundred and seventy-five (1875), the amount of forty per cent. of the gross earnings received from the demised premises, and, after the expiration of said three years and during the remainder of the term, the rent shall be paid as reserved in said lease if the rent so reserved is sufficient to pay said coupons, but if not sufficient to pay said coupons, then the Wisconsin Central Railroad Company shall pay, and the Milwaukee and Northern Railway Company shall accept, in full satisfaction of rent for the demised premises, such part of said gross earnings, not exceeding in any event forty per cent. thereof, as shall be sufficient to pay said coupons, all accounts being settled exactly, and all liabilities and obligations between the two companies being adjusted and discharged by and upon the semi-annual statements provided in said lease, and on the

74   thirty-first day of May and the thirtieth day of November in each year, and said semi-annual statements being accepted by each company as final adjustments of all claims for rent of the demised premises to the respective dates thereof.

Second. Taxes, from and after the first day of January, A. D. eighteen hundred and eighty (1880), shall not be deducted from the gross receipts before computation of rent for the demised premises, but shall thenceforward be borne and paid by the lessee as part of the operating expenses.

Third. The Milwaukee and Northern Railway Company hereby agrees to perform prior to December first, A. D. eighteen hundred and seventy-six (1876), all its agreements in reference to the demised premises which are at this date unfulfilled, and to complete without unnecessary delay the various structures which are on its part contemplated to be built under provisions of said lease and schedules, and also hereby agrees that if the same be not finished prior to the first day of December, A. D. 1876, then the lessee is hereby authorized to complete the same forthwith at the expense of the lessor and to apply to this purpose, so far as is necessary for such completion, any surplus rent, after payment of the coupons aforesaid, which shall be then or thereafter earned.

Fourth. The Milwaukee and Northern Railway Company, in consideration of the increased rental and agreements aforesaid on the part of the Wisconsin Central Railroad Company, hereby releases the Wisconsin Central Railroad Company from any and all obligation to hereafter make any advances of money to take up the interest coupons of the Milwaukee and Northern Railway Company, as stipulated in said lease, and also from any and every obligation and liability arising out of any previous neglect to make said advances hitherto due and payable under terms of said lease, and also from any and every obligation to pay any money under said lease and any provision thereof in the nature of rent and advances to or for the benefit of the Milwaukee and Northern Railway Company, except the proportion of gross earnings (not exceeding in any event forty per cent. thereof) which is herein agreed, when and as the same is payable under terms of this agreement and said' lease.

75   Fifth. If any difference of opinion arise as to the performance by either party of its covenants contained in said lease and in this agreement said difference shall be submitted to three competent arbitrators, who shall be jointly selected by the parties, or, in default of such selection within sixty days after written request therefor, shall be appointed on the application of either party, after ten days' notice in writing to the other party, by any judge of the circuit court of the United States having for the time being jurisdiction in this district or of some United States court succeeding said court in said district. And it is further agreed that the written award of said arbitrators, or a majority of the same, made after due notice to and hearing of both parties and their witnesses, shall have the legal effect of an award.

Sixth. All the provisions of said lease, except so far as the same are herein expressly modified or changed, are hereby by each of said companies ratified and confirmed, and all causes of action for breach of any agreement therein contained, which have arisen from its date of execution until this day, are hereby mutually waived and forever released by and between said companies.

In witness whereof the parties hereto have caused these presents to be signed respectively by Angus Smith, vice-president of the Milwaukee and Northern Railway Company, for and in behalf of the Milwaukee and Northern Railway Company, and by Gardner Colby, president of the Wisconsin Central Railroad Company, for and in behalf of the Wisconsin Central Railroad Company, they being thereunto lawfully authorized so to do, and the seals of the said companies to be hereto affixed this first day of June, A. D. eighteen hundred and seventy-five, in the city of Milwaukee and State of Wisconsin.

(Signed)   THE MILWAUKEE AND NORTHERN
                    RAILWAY COMPANY,
[SEAL.]   By ANGUS SMITH, *Vice-President*.
(Signed)   THE WISCONSIN CENTRAL RAIL-
                    ROAD COMPANY,
[SEAL.]   By GARDNER COLBY, *President*.

In presence of—
(Signed)   E. MARINER.
                L. S. DIXON.

76   STATE OF WISCONSIN,   } *ss*:
            County of Milwaukee,

MILWAUKEE, *June 2d*, 1875.

Personally appeared Gardner Colby, president of the Wisconsin Central Railroad Company, and Angus Smith, vice-president of the

Milwaukee and Northern Railway Company, and severally acknowledged the foregoing instrument to be the free act and deed of their respective corporations.

Before me—

[SEAL.]   (Signed)   F. W. WEBSTER,
                                                Notary Public.

Exhibit "D."

Agreement made the tenth day of October, A. D. eighteen hundred and seventy-six, by and between the Milwaukee and Northern Railway Company; Jesse Hoyt and A. Warren Greenleaf, trustees; James Ludington, Guido Pfister, Angus Smith, and Jesse Hoyt, parties of the first part, and the Wisconsin Central Railroad Company, party of the second part:

Whereas, on the eighth day of November, A. D. eighteen hundred and seventy-three, the Milwaukee and Northern Railway Company executed to and with the Wisconsin Central Railroad Company an indenture of lease of the Milwaukee and Northern railroad, wherein the Wisconsin Marine and Fire Insurance Company Bank was appointed a trustee for certain purposes therein declared;

And whereas, on the first day of June, A. D. eighteen hundred and seventy-five, said corporations executed a supplemental agreement modifying said lease, and subsequently, on the same day, executed an additional agreement, whereby Jesse Hoyt, of the city of New York, was appointed temporary trustee under said lease so as aforesaid modified, for the period of twelve months, which period has now expired;

And whereas said Jesse Hoyt and A. Warren Greenleaf,
77   trustees of the first mortgage and bonds of the Milwaukee
       and Northern Railway Company, have heretofore instituted against said company a suit in equity in the circuit court of the United States for the eastern district of Wisconsin for the foreclosure of said mortgage and bonds, and are now entitled, at their option, to take a decree against said Milwaukee and Northern Railway Company and evict said company from said railway and all other property covered by said mortgage and lease;

And whereas said James Ludington has heretofore instituted against the Milwaukee and Northern Railway Company a suit in the circuit court of Milwaukee county, in the State of Wisconsin, wherein he has obtained a judgment of foreclosure and sale against said company;

And whereas, on the 27th day of December, A. D. eighteen hundred and seventy-five, all the franchises of the Milwaukee and Northern Railway Company and all its property, records, and writings, together with said lease of said railway, was in pursuance of said judgment sold at public auction by the sheriff of said Milwaukee county;

And whereas Guido Pfister, Angus Smith, James Ludington, and Jesse Hoyt allege some claim or title, legal or equitable, jointly [or] severally, in and to the premises, under and by virtue of said sale, or otherwise;

And whereas all the parties interested in the premises desire the appointment of a trustee under said lease so as aforesaid modified, without prejudice to the legal rights of either party in the premises:

Now, therefore, the parties of the first part severally declare that no person or corporation not now joined in this agreement is, to the best of their knowledge, information, and belief, in any way interested, or asserts any rights, title, or interest in and to the premises, or any part thereof, and they severally request the party of the second part to assent to the appointment of Jesse Hoyt as trustee under said lease so as aforesaid modified, and hereby declare that
78   any and all receipts given by said Hoyt for any and all moneys to him paid by the lessee on account of the rental reserved in said lease so as aforesaid modified shall be a full quittance to the lessee therefor and an absolute bar in favor of said lessee against any and all persons whatsoever claiming the same, and the said parties of the first part jointly and severally covenant to hold said lessee harmless against any and all claim at any time hereafter made by any person or corporation whatsoever as to the moneys so paid to said Hoyt as trustee.

And all the parties hereto do hereby agree and consent that Jesse Hoyt, of the city, county, and State of New York, be, and hereby is, appointed trustee under said lease and supplemental agreement and shall so continue until ninety days after written notice shall have been given by any one or more of the parties herein named to said Hoyt of their desire to appoint a new trustee in his place, and that said Hoyt shall, at the expiration of ninety days after said notice has been given, cease to be such trustee, whereupon all the rights of the several parties hereto shall be the same as if this agreement had never been made.

And Jesse Hoyt hereby accepts said trust and agrees that during the time he shall be trustee as aforesaid either party to said lease may, in the name of, but without any expense to, said Hoyt, use his name as trustee in any legal proceedings which said party may desire to institute in order to obtain the decision of the United States circuit court upon the construction of said lease or administration of said trust.

In testimony whereof the Milwaukee and Northern Railway Company has caused these presents to be sealed with its common seal and to be signed by Jesse Hoyt, its president, for and in behalf of said company, and said Jesse Hoyt and A. Warren Greenleaf, trustees; Guido Pfister, Angus Smith, James Ludington, and Jesse Hoyt have hereto set their hands and seals, and said Wisconsin Central
79   Railroad Company has caused these presents to be sealed with its corporate seal and to be signed by Charles L. Colby, its vice-president, for and in behalf of said company, the day and year first above written.

MILWAUKEE AND NORTHERN
RAILWAY CO.,

(Signed)   By JESSE HOYT, *President.*
(Signed)   JESSE HOYT, *Trustee.*   [SEAL.]
            A. W. GREENLEAF, *Trustee.*   [SEAL.]
            JAMES LUDINGTON, *Trustee.*   [SEAL.]

80 · Exhibit "E."

This indenture, made this seventh day of January, 1878, by and between The Milwaukee & Northern Railway Company, of the first part, and Jesse Hoyt and A. Warren Greenleaf, of the second part witnesseth:

That the said party of the first part, in order further to secure the payment of its first-mortgage bonds, hereby sells, assigns, and sets over unto the said parties of the second part a certain indenture of lease bearing date November 8th, 1878, executed by and between the said party of the first part and The Wisconsin Central Railroad Company for the lease of said first party's railway and the payment of the rent therefor, and all and singular the covenants of said Wisconsin Central Railroad Company in said lease contained, and in each and every modification thereof, and all moneys due or to grow due thereon, upon the very same trusts, however, as are expressed in a certain trust-deed heretofore executed by the party of the first part to the parties of the second part as security for the first-mortgage bonds of the party of the first part, which said deed bears date the first day of December, 1870, and is recorded in the office of the secretary of state of the State of Wisconsin, in vol. three of mortgages, pages twenty-six to thirty-seven, inclusive.

In testimony whereof the said party of the first part has
81   caused these presents to be subscribed by its vice-president and countersigned by its secretary and sealed with its corporate seal the day and year first above written

[Seal M. & N. R'y Co.]

ANGUS SMITH, *Vice-President.*

Attest: WM. TAINTOR, *Secretary.*

Signed, sealed, and delivered in presence of—
   E. MARINER.
   FRANK M. HOYT.

Exhibit "F."

MILWAUKEE, WIS., *Jan. 8th*, 1878.

The Wisconsin Central Railway Company—Charles L. Colby, president.

DEAR SIR: You will please take notice that the lease between the Milwaukee and Northern Railway Company and your company, and all modifications thereof, and all rents due and to grow due thereon, and all the covenants in such lease and the modifications thereof have been assigned to us upon the trusts contained in the mortgage deed to us to secure the first-mortgage bonds, and that you are expected to pay over the rents to Mr. Jesse Hoyt, as you have heretofore paid them, such assignment being intended merely as further security for said bonds and not to disturb the rela-
82   tions of the parties to such lease and modifications.
   Yours, etc.,   JESSE HOYT AND
                           A. WARREN GREENLEAF,
   (Signed)   By E. MARINER, *Their Attorney.*

83   " EXHIBIT G." .

Circuit Court of the United States, Eastern District of Wisconsin.

JESSE HOYT, Surviving Trustee,
against
THE MILWAUKEE & NORTHERN RAILWAY COMPANY and THE WIS-
CONSIN CENTRAL RAILROAD COMPANY.

The application of the complainant for a receiver in the above-
entitled cause coming on this day to be heard, upon motion of the
said complainant and the stipulation of all the parties, made in open
court:

It is hereby ordered and adjudged that James C. Spencer be, and
hereby is, appointed receiver of all and singular the property, estate,
and effects of the said Milwaukee & Northern Railway Company
particularly described in the trust-deed set forth in the bill of complaint in this cause.

And it is further ordered that the said James C. Spencer, before
entering upon the duties of his said office, enter into a bond with
sufficient sureties, to be approved by one of the judges of said court,
in the penal sum of fifty thousand dollars, for the faithful discharge
of his duties as such receiver.

And it is further ordered and adjudged that each and every of
the parties to this proceeding, their agents, servants, attorneys, and
84   all parties claiming by, through, or under them, subsequent to the bringing of this suit, their officers, agents, servants, and attorneys, upon demand of said receiver for them,
make over to him all and singular said property, estate, and effects
described in and by said mortgage, and all and singular the books,
papers, maps, plans, and vouchers in their or either of their possession or control at any time the property of said Milwaukee & Northern Railway Company pertaining to the aforesaid property, estate,
and effects.

And it is further ordered and adjudged that the agreement of
lease heretofore entered into by and between the Milwaukee and
Northern Railway Company and the Wisconsin Central Railroad
Company, bearing date the eighth day of November, 1873, and the
agreements in modification thereof, shall be and hereby are declared
cancelled and annulled as to all future transactions, including all
future transactions with the trustees of the first mortgage of the
Wisconsin Central Railroad Company : Provided, That the trustees
of the Wisconsin Central Railroad Company, Edwin H. Abbot and
John A. Stewart, shall turn over the property and premises mentioned in said agreement of lease, in their or either of their possession or control, to such receiver, such cancellation and nullification
85   to take effect upon such premises and property being turned
over as aforesaid.

It is further ordered that the said James C. Spencer at once,
upon entering upon the said duties of his office, make a full and
complete inventory of all and singular the property and estate of
said company which shall come into his hands, and that he state

the condition of the railway and rolling-stock of said company, and that he report without delay, and that said receiver continue the operation of said railroad personally or through such agents or servants as he shall appoint, and that such receiver from time to time have leave to take the direction of this court as to the manner of the management of said property and the performance of his duties as such receiver.

CHAS. E. DYER, *Judge.*

Exhibit "H."

New York City, N. Y., *Jan'y 11th,* '79.

Jesse Hoyt, Esq., president of the Milwaukee and Northern Railway Company, and surviving trustee under its first mortgage and bonds, and trustee under its lease of its railway to the Wisconsin Central Railway Company, and assignee of said lease under assignment thereof.

Dear Sir: We beg to inform you that on the third day of January current we, as trustees under and by virtue of the provisions of 86 the first mortgage of the Wisconsin Central Railroad Company, entered upon and took possession of the property covered by that mortgage, and are now operating the Wisconsin Central railroad.

We find that said company was operating the Milwaukee and Northern railway under a lease. We are not sufficiently informed upon the subject to warrant us in assuming any obligation under that lease. We therefore notify you that we decline to assume, affirm, or in any way ratify that lease. We wish, however, not to interfere in any way with the welfare of that railway, and, unless you otherwise elect, will continue for the present to operate the same temporarily for such compensation as that service may be fairly worth, and, as far as is necessary, but not in excess of its earnings, to repair the same as the Wisconsin Central Railroad Company was doing, and also to permit the business of the Wisconsin Central Railroad Company to be done as heretofore over that railway. We suggest that you arrange for an early personal interview with us, at which you will make known to us your wishes, and confer with a view to a more permanent arrangement.

We are ready to submit to the parties in interest any proposition which yourself and we are jointly able to recommend.

We are, very respectfully, your obedient servants,

(Signed) JOHN A. STEWART,
EDWIN H. ABBOT,
Trustees.

87 ### Exhibit "I."

Upon accounting together it is agreed by and between John A. Stewart and Edwin H. Abbot, as trustees of the Wisconsin Central railroad, and Jesse Hoyt, as trustee of the Milwaukee and Northern Railway Company, and surviving trustee under its first mortgage and bonds, and trustee under its lease of its railway to the Wisconsin Railroad Company, and assignee of said lease under assignment thereof, that the sum of twenty-eight thousand two hundred and fifty-eight dollars and forty-four cents is the amount payable by said trustees to the party lawfully entitled to receive the same out of the moneys received by said trustees from the operation of the Milwaukee and Northern railway since the third day of January, A. D. 1879, to the first day of May, A. D. 1879, in full settlement of all accounts between said trustees and said Hoyt as aforesaid, arising out of said trustees' operation of said railway during said period.

And the said Jesse Hoyt hereby acknowledges the payment of said sum.

Milwaukee, July 23, 1879.

JESSE HOYT,

Trustee as aforesaid,

By ANGUS SMITH.

JOHN A. STEWART AND

E. H. ABBOT, *Trustees,*

By CHAS. L. COLBY, *Agent.*

88   EXHIBIT "J."

Know all men by these presents that we, Angus Smith, Guido Pfister, and Ephraim Mariner, all of the city of Milwaukee and State of Wisconsin, are held and firmly bound unto John A. Stewart of the city of New York, and Edwin H. Abbot, of the city of Cambridge, in the State of Massachusetts, in the sum of sixty thousand dollars, lawful money of the United States of America, to be paid to the said John A. Stewart and Edwin H. Abbot, or to their certain attorneys and their heirs, executors, administrators, or assigns; to which payment, well and truly to be made, we bind ourselves and our heirs, executors, and administrators, and each and every of them, jointly and severally, firmly by these presents.

Sealed with our seals and dated the 22nd day of July, in the year of our Lord one thousand eight hundred and seventy-nine.

Whereas the above-named John A. Stewart and Edwin H. Abbot operated the railroad called the Milwaukee and Northern railway from about the third day of January, 1879, until the first day of May, 1879, and during said term received the earnings of said railroad;

And whereas it has been ascertained on an accounting that after the payment of all expenses the balance remaining in the hands of said Stewart and Abbot, due to the owners of said railway or to the parties entitled to receive the same, is the sum of twenty-eight thousand six hundred and sixty-four dollars and five cents ($28,664.05);

And whereas, on or about the 30th day of November, 1875, the Brooks Locomotive Works, by De Witt Davis, their attorney, recovered a judgment in the circuit court of the United States for the eastern district of Wisconsin against the said Milwaukee and Northern Railway Company for the sum of fifteen thousand three hundred and sixty-eight dollars and seventy-two cents, and said Brooks Locomotive Works have caused the said John A. Stewart and Edwin H. Abbot, as trustees and individually, to be garnished as having in their possession or control property belonging to said railway company;

And whereas one Jesse Hoyt, of the city of New York,
89   claims to be entitled to receive said money hereinbefore
named, and at his request and at the request of the obligors hereto, the said Stewart and Abbot have paid to him the said sum of twenty-eight thousand six hundred and sixty-four dollars and five cents ($28,664.05):

Now, therefore, the condition of this obligation is such that if the said Jesse Hoyt, his heirs, executors, or administrators, or any of them, shall pay any judgment, order, or decree which may be entered or obtained against said John A. Stewart and Edwin H. Abbot, or either of them, by reason of paying over said money to said Hoyt, and shall well and truly indemnify and save harmless, and keep the said John A. Stewart and Edwin H. Abbot and their heirs, executors, administrators, or assigns indemnified and saved harmless of and from all obligations, damages, costs, expenses, charges, fees, suits, actions, judgments, and executions that may at any time arise or be brought against them, or either of them, by reason of paying over said sum of money to said Hoyt, then this obligation shall be void; else valid.

E. MARINER.   [SEAL.]
GUIDO PFISTER.   [SEAL.]
ANGUS SMITH.   [SEAL.]

90   And same day (May 21, 1883) came the defendant, The
Milwaukee & Northern Railway Company, by its counsel, Mr. Mariner, and moved the court for a new trial for reasons filed, as follows:

Motion for a New Trial.

Circuit Court of the United States, Eastern District of Wisconsin.

THE BROOKS LOCOMOTIVE WORKS

vs.

THE MILWAUKEE & NORTHERN RAILWAY COMPANY; JOHN A. STEWART & EDWIN H. ABBOT, Garnishees.

And now comes the said defendant, and, upon the minutes of the court and the record and proceeding in the above action and the finding of the court, moves a new trial of the action.

E. MARINER,
Att'y for the Def't.

AUGUST 25, 1883.

This day came the defendant, The Milwaukee & Northern Railway Co., by its attorney, and filed its exceptions to the findings, as follows:

Exceptions to Finding.

Circuit Court of the United States for the Eastern District of Wisconsin.

THE BROOKS LOCOMOTIVE WORKS
vs.
THE MILWAUKEE AND NORTHERN RAILWAY COMPANY; STEWART and ABBOTT, Garnishees.

91   And now comes The Milwaukee and Northern Railway Company, by E. Mariner, its attorney, and excepts to the finding of facts; that it omits to find that the garnishees took possession of The Milwaukee and Northern Railway Company's railroad under The Wisconsin Central Co., and further excepts to the conclusions of law of the court in the above-entitled cause and to each and every of them, so far as either of them finds that, as matter of law, there was a fund accumulated in the hands of the garnishees from any source which was property of the principal defendant, and which could be attached as its property.

Second. The said defendant further excepts to the second conclusion of law of said court that the trustees were not liable to The Wisconsin Central company for the use and occupation of The Milwaukee and Northern road after their entry and up to the date of their lease from the receiver.

Third. The defendant excepts to the conclusion of law that the occupation of the trustees was not under the lease from The Milwaukee and Northern Railway Company to The Wisconsin Central Railroad Company, but was in defiance thereof and in opposition thereto.

92   Fourth. The defendant excepts to the fourth conclusion of law that the amount agreed upon between Stewart and Abbot, the garnishees, and Hoyt, as trustee under said lease and assignee thereof, was property of The Milwaukee and Northern Railway Company, liable to be attached for its debts, and that it was attached by the service of the process in this cause.

Fifth. The defendant excepts to the conclusion of law that at the time of the service of the process in this cause the garnishees had in their hands belonging to the defendant, The Milwaukee and Northern Railway Company, the sum of twenty-eight thousand two hundred and fifty-eight dollars and forty-four cents.

Sixth. The defendant, The Milwaukee and Northern Railway Company, excepts to the conclusion of law that the garnishees were indebted to it in the sum of twenty-eight thousand two hundred and fifty-eight dollars and forty-four cents, or any other sum.

Seventh. The said defendant excepts to the conclusion of law that the plaintiff was entitled to judgment against the said garnishees for the sum of twenty-three thousand four hundred and ten dollars and forty cents, or for any sum whatever.

Eighth. The said defendant excepts to the order that judgment be entered against the garnishees.

E. MARINER,
Att'y for Principal Defendant.

93   And now at this same term, to wit, July special term, 1883, and on the fourth day thereof, to wit, on the 1st day of September, A. D. 1883, the following proceedings were had, to wit:

Motion for New Trial Overruled, & Judgment.

The Brooks Locomotive Works ⎫
vs. ⎪
The Milwaukee & Northern Railway Co., Defendant; ⎪ At Law.
   The Wisconsin Central Railroad Company, Charles ⎬
   L. Colby, Edwin H. Abbot, and John A. Stewart & Edwin H. Abbot, Trustees, as Garnishees. ⎭

This day come the parties by their counsel, and the motion of the defendant, The Milwaukee & Northern Railway Company, for a new trial having been heretofore argued and submitted, on consideration thereof it is ordered by the court that said motion be, and hereby is, overruled.

Whereupon, on motion of Davis, Riess & Shepard, counsel for the plaintiff, it is considered and adjudged by this court now here that this cause be, and hereby is, dismissed as to the garnishees, The Wisconsin Central Railroad Company and Charles L. Colby, and that the said plaintiff do have and recover of Edwin H. Abbot and John A. Stewart, garnishees of the defendant, The Milwaukee & Northern

94   Railway Company, the sum of twenty-three thousand four hundred and ten dollars and forty cents, pursuant to the finding

of the court, with interest thereon from May 21, 1883, to this date, amounting to four hundred and fifty-five dollars and twenty cents, and amounting in all to twenty-three thousand eight hundred and sixty-five dollars and sixty cents, together with fifty-one dollars and twenty-six cents, its costs about its said suit in this behalf by it expended, and that it have execution therefor.

Judgment-roll signed September 1st, A. D. 1883.

EDWARD KURTZ, *Clerk.*

Damages ____ $23,865.60
Costs _____   51.26
            ―――――――
         $23,916.86

NOVEMBER 3, 1883.

This day came Guido Pfister, Angus Smith, and Ephraim Mariner, and filed their bond in the sum of fifty thousand dollars, conditioned that the garnishees, John A. Stewart and Edwin H. Abbot, trustees, shall prosecute a writ of error to effect and answer all damages and costs if they fail to make their plea good, which bond is approved by the district judge and is as follows, to wit:

Supersedeas Bond.

Know all men by these presents that we, Guido Pfister,
95   Angus Smith, and Ephraim Mariner, are held and firmly bound unto The Brooks Locomotive Works in the sum of fifty thousand dollars, lawful money, to be paid to the said The

Brooks Locomotive Works, its successors and assigns; to which payment, well and truly to be made, we bind ourselves, our executors, administrators, & heirs, jointly & severally, firmly by these presents.

Sealed with our seals and dated this second day of November, 1883.

Whereas The Brooks Locomotive Works, the obligee above named, on the first day of September, 1883, in a certain suit then pending in the circuit court of the United States for the eastern district of Wisconsin, wherein The Brooks Locomotive Works was plaintiff, and The Milwaukee and Northern Railway Company principal defendant—The Wisconsin Central Railroad Company, Charles L. Colby, Edwin H. Abbot, and John A. Stewart and Edwin H. Abbot, trustees, garnishees of the said principal defendant the said The Milwaukee and Northern Railway Company, defendant—recovered judgment against said defendant, The Milwaukee and Northern Railway Company, and said John A. Stewart and Edwin H. Abbot, as trustees, as such garnishees, that the plaintiff do have and recover

96   from said Stewart and Abbot, trustees and garnishees, the sum of twenty-three thousand nine hundred and sixteen dollars and eighty-six cents, damages and costs;

And whereas the said John A. Stewart and Edwin H. Abbot, feeling aggrieved thereby, have sued out a writ of error to the Supreme Court of the United States:

Now, therefore, the condition of the foregoing obligation is such that if the said defendants shall prosecute such writ of error to effect, and if they fail to make their plea good shall answer all damages and costs, then this obligation shall be null & void; otherwise of force.

EPHRAIM MARINER.   [L. S.]
ANGUS SMITH.   [L. S.]
GUIDO PFISTER.   [L. S.]

EASTERN DISTRICT OF WISCONSIN, ss:

This second day of November, 1883, before me came Angus Smith, Guido Pfister, & Ephraim Mariner and made oath, each for himself, that he was a freeholder in said district, and was worth the sum of fifty thousand dollars over and above all liabilities and exemptions.

EDWARD KURTZ, Clerk.

Endorsed: Approved Nov. 3, 1883.   C. E. Dyer, judge.

97   Whereupon it is ordered by the court that execution be superseded and a writ of error and citation issued, and a copy of said writ of error lodged for the defendant in error.

And same day (November 3, 1883) came the said Guido Pfister, Angus Smith, and Ephraim Mariner and filed their bond in the sum of five hundred dollars, conditioned that the defendant, The Milwaukee & Northern Railway Company, shall prosecute a writ of error to effect and answer all costs if it fail to make its plea good, which bond is approved by the district judge, and is as follows:

Bond on Behalf of Mil. & N. R'y Co. for Costs on Writ of Error.

Know all men by these presents that we, Guido Pfister, Angus Smith, and Ephraim Mariner, are held and firmly bound unto The Brooks Locomotive Works in the sum of five hundred dollars, lawful money, to be paid to the said The Brooks Locomotive Works, its successors and assigns; to which payment, well and truly to be made, we bind ourselves, our executors, administrators, & heirs, firmly by these presents.

Sealed with our seals and dated this second day of November, 1883.

Whereas the Brooks Locomotive Works, the obligee above named, on the first day of September, 1883, in a certain suit then pending in the circuit court of the United States for the eastern district of Wisconsin, wherein the Brooks Locomotive Works was plaintiff and the Milwaukee and Northern Railway Company principal defendant—the Wisconsin Central Railroad Company, Charles L. Colby, Edwin H. Abbot, and John A. Stewart and Edwin H. Abbot, trustees, garnishees of the said principal defendant, the said The Milwaukee and Northern Railway Company, defendant—recovered judgment against said defendant, The Milwaukee and Northern Railway Company, and said John A. Stewart and Edwin H. Abbot, as trustees, as such garnishees, that the plaintiff do have and recover from said Stewart and Abbot, trustees and garnishees, the sum of twenty-three thousand nine hundred and sixteen dollars and eighty-six cents, damages and costs;

And whereas the said Milwaukee and Northern Railway Company, feeling aggrieved thereby, have sued out a writ of error to the Supreme Court of the United States:

Now, therefore, the condition of the foregoing obligation is such that if the said defendant shall prosecute such writ of error to effect, and if it fail to make its plea good shall answer all costs, then this obligation shall be null & void; otherwise of force.

EPHRAIM MARINER. [L. S.]
ANGUS SMITH. [L. S.]
GUIDO PFISTER. [L. S.]

99   EASTERN DISTRICT OF WISCONSIN, *ss:*

This third day of November, 1883, before me came Angus Smith, Guido Pfister, & Ephraim Mariner and made oath, each for himself, that he was a freeholder in the State of Wisconsin, in said district, and was worth the sum of one thousand dollars over and above all debts, liabilities, & exemptions.

EDWARD KURTZ, *Clerk.*

Endorsed: Approved Nov. 3, 1883.   C. E. Dyer, judge.

Whereupon a writ of error and citation issued, and a copy of said writ of error lodged for the defendant in error.

100   UNITED STATES OF AMERICA, } *ss:*
           Eastern District of Wisconsin, }

I, Edward Kurtz, clerk of the circuit court of the United States of America for the eastern district of Wisconsin, do hereby certify that I have compared the writings annexed to this certificate with their originals now on file and remaining of record in my office, and that they are true copies of such originals and correct transcripts therefrom, being a full and complete transcript of the record in the case of The Brooks Locomotive Works *vs.* The Milwaukee & Northern Railway Co., defendant, and The Wisconsin Central R. R. Co. *et al.*, garnishees.

In testimony whereof I have hereunto set my hand and duly affixed the seal of the said court at the city of Milwaukee, in said district, this 19th day of December, in the year of our Lord one thousand eight hundred and eighty-three, and of the Independence of the United States the 108th.

[Seal U. S. Circuit Court, Eastern District Wisconsin.]

· EDWARD KURTZ, *Clerk.*

101   UNITED STATES OF AMERICA, *ss :*

The President of the United States of America to the judges of the circuit court of the United States of America for the eastern district of Wisconsin, Greeting :

[Seal U. S. Circuit Court, Eastern District Wisconsin.]

Because in the record and proceedings as also in the rendition of a judgment in a plea which is in the said circuit court of the United States of America for the eastern district of Wisconsin, before you, between The Brooks Locomotive Works, plaintiff, and The Milwaukee & Northern Railway Company, defendant, and The Wisconsin Central Railroad Company, Charles L. Colby, Edwin H. Abbot, and John A. Stewart & Edwin H. Abbot, trustees, as garnishees, defendant-, a manifest error hath happened, to the great damage of the said John A. Stewart & Edwin H. Abbot, trustees, as garnishees, as by the complaint appears, and it being fit that the error, if any there hath been, should be duly corrected and full and speedy justice done to the parties aforesaid in this behalf, you are hereby commanded, if judgment be therein given, that then, under your seal, distinctly and openly, you send the record and proceedings aforesaid, with all things concerning the same, to the Supreme Court of the United States, together with this writ, so that you have the same at Washington on the second Monday of October next in the Supreme Court to be there and then held, that, the record and proceedings aforesaid being inspected, the said Supreme Court may cause further to be done therein to correct that error that of right and according to the law and custom of the United States should be done.

Witness the Honorable Morrison R. Waite, Chief Justice of the said Supreme Court of the United States, this third day of November, in the year of our Lord one thousand eight hundred and eighty-three, and of the Independence of the United States the 108th.

EDWARD KURTZ,
Clerk U. S. Circuit Court, East'n Dist. of Wisconsin.

102   THE UNITED STATES OF AMERICA, *ss:*

[SEAL.]   To The Brooks Locomotive Works, Greeting:

You are hereby cited and admonished to be and appear at a Supreme Court of the United States to be holden at Washington on the second Monday of October next, pursuant to a writ of error filed in the clerk's office of the circuit court of the United States for the eastern district of Wisconsin, wherein John A. Stewart and Edwin H. Abbot, trustees, as garnishees, are plaintiffs in error, and you are defendant in error, to show cause, if any there be, why the judgment in the said writ of error mentioned should not be corrected, and speedy justice should not be done to the parties in that behalf.

Witness the Honorable Charles E. Dyer, district judge of the United States for the eastern district of Wisconsin, at the city of Milwaukee, in said district, this third day of November, A. D. 1883, and of the Independence of the United States the 108th.

CHAS. E. DYER, *Judge.*

I accept service of the above citation this 22nd day of November, A. D. 1883.

DE WITT DAVIS,
Attorney for Defendant in Error.

103   UNITED STATES OF AMERICA, *ss:*

The President of the United States of America to the judges of the circuit court of the United States of America for the eastern district of Wisconsin, Greeting:

[Seal U. S. Circuit Court, Eastern District Wisconsin.]

Because in the record and proceedings as also in the rendition of a judgment in a plea which is in the said circuit court of the United States of America for the eastern district of Wisconsin, before you, between The Brooks Locomotive Works, plaintiff, and The Milwaukee & Northern Railway Company, defendant, and The Wisconsin Central Railroad Company, Charles L. Colby, Edwin H. Abbot, and John A. Stewart & Edwin H. Abbot, trustees, as garnishees, defendant, a manifest error hath happened, to the great damage of the said Milwaukee & Northern Railway Company, defendant, as by the complaint appears, and it being fit that the error, if any there hath been, should be duly corrected and full and speedy justice done to the parties aforesaid in this behalf, you are hereby commanded, if judgment be therein given, that then, under your seal, distinctly and openly, you send the record and proceedings aforesaid, with all things concerning the same, to the Supreme Court of the United States, together with this writ, so that you have the same at Washington on the second Monday of October next in the Supreme Court to be then and there held, that, the record and proceedings aforesaid being inspected, the said Supreme Court may cause further to be done therein to correct that error that of right and according to the law and custom of the United States should be done.

8—226

Witness the Honorable Morrison R. Waite, Chief Justice of the said Supreme Court of the United States, this third day of November, in the year of our Lord one thousand eight hundred and eighty-three, and of the Independence of the United States the 108th.

EDWARD KURTZ,
Clerk U. S. Circuit Court, East'n Dist. of Wisconsin.

104   THE UNITED STATES OF AMERICA, *ss*:

[SEAL.]   To the Brooks Locomotive Works, Greeting:

You are hereby cited and admonished to be and appear at a Supreme Court of the United States to be holden at Washington on the second Monday of October next, pursuant to a writ of error filed in the clerk's office of the circuit court of the United States for the eastern district of Wisconsin, wherein The Milwaukee and Northern Railway Company is plaintiff in error and you are defendant in error to show cause, if any there be, why the judgment in the said writ of error mentioned should not be corrected, and speedy justice should not be done to the parties in that behalf.

Witness the Honorable Charles E. Dyer, district judge of the United States for the eastern district of Wisconsin, at the city of Milwaukee, in said district, this third day of November, A. D. 1883, and of the Independence of the United States the 108th.

CHAS. E. DYER, *Judge.*

I accept service of the above citation this 22nd day of November, A. D. 1883.

DE WITT DAVIS,
Attorney for Defendant in Error.

Endorsed on cover: E. Wisconsin C. C. U. S.   No. 226.   The Milwaukee & Northern Railway Company, plaintiff in error, *vs.* The Brooks Locomotive Works.   Filed 19th January, 1884.

SUPREME COURT OF THE UNITED STATES,

OCTOBER TERM, 1886.

THE MILWAUKEE & NORTHERN RAIL-
ROAD COMPANY *et al.*, *Pl'ff's in Error*,

vs.

No. 226.

THE BROOKS LOCOMOTIVE WORKS, *Def't
in Error.*

E. MARINER,
Attorney for Plaintiff in Error.

R O POLKINHORN PRINTER

SUPREME COURT OF THE UNITED STATES.

OCTOBER TERM, 1886.

THE MILWAUKEE & NORTHERN RAIL-
ROAD COMPANY *et al., Pl'ff's in Error,*

vs. No. 226.

THE BROOKS LOCOMOTIVE WORKS, *Def't*
in Error.

This is an appeal from a judgment of the Circuit
Court of the Eastern District of Wisconsin in a,
statutory action of garnishment after execution, to
attach a supposed joint liability of the garnishees,
Stewart and Abbott, as trustees, in a mortgage made
by the Wisconsin Central Railroad Company which
I shall call the Central Company, to the Milwaukee
and Northern Railroad Company which I shall call
the Northern Company, for the rent or the use and
occupation of the Northern Road.

The Northern Company was organized under chap.
94 of the private and local laws of Wisconsin for
1870, to build a road from Milwaukee to the Fox
River below Lake Winnebago, and thence to Lake
Superior.

The Wisconsin Central Company was organized
under ch. 314 and 362, P. and L. laws, Wis., 1866,
ch. 257, laws 1869 and ch. 27 of laws of 1871, to

build a road from Doty's Island in Fox River below Lake Winnebago by way of Stevens' Point, to Ashland upon Lake Superior. Both roads were mortgaged to trustees.

When the Northern Road was completed so as to meet the Central, the Central Company, in order to get a through line to Milwaukee, leased the Northern road for 999 years by a lease (Ex. B. fol. 66) for a rent which was a percentage of the gross earnings graduated according to the amount of money earned. The lease provided that the rent should be paid monthly, on the first of the second month after the money was earned; December rent the first of February; January rent the first of March, etc.; and that the rent be paid "to such trustee as shall be from time to time jointly selected by the parties hereto upon the trust to keep the same until the next installment of interest is due upon the bonds issued by the first party (the Northern Co.) under their first mortgage, and then apply the same or so much thereof as shall be necessary to the payment of said interest when and as payable, and if any surplus remain after payment of said interest to pay the same to the first party. (Finding fol. 68). The Wisconsin Marine and Fire Insurance Company Bank was made first trustee in the lease.

At that time there was no statute in Wisconsin enabling a railroad company to lease its road and franchises.

By sec. 1, chapter 292, of the laws of 1874, any railroad company whose line was wholly in Wisconsin, as the Central Company's was, was authorized to lease any other railroad with its franchises, etc.

The rent was not sufficient to pay the interest upon the bonds of the Northern Co., and the trustee in the mortgage brought a suit to foreclose it against both companies. (6 Finding, fol. 41.)

Afterwards, in June, 1875, the companies made an agreement modifying the lease, increasing the rent and confirming the lease, except as modified (Ex. C. to Findings). After this agreement, this suit slept till the garnishees took possession of the Northern road.

October 10, 1876, a subsequent agreement was made between the two companies, and Hoyt and Greenleaf as trustees in the Northern Company's mortgage, Ludington, a judgment creditor, Pfister, a purchaser of the road, at a sale on a bill filed for the sale of the road, and Hoyt, providing that all payments of rent shall be made to Hoyt as trustee, and appointing him trustee under the lease, and that all payments made to him on account of the rental reserved by the lease as modified should be "a full acquittance to the lessee and an absolute bar in favor of said lessee against any and all persons whatsoever claiming the same."

From that time to the time of the entry by the garnishees the Central Company paid the rent to Hoyt as trustee.

In January, 1878, the Northern Company assigned this lease, as modified, to Hoyt and Greenleaf, trustees in the mortgage of the Northern Company as further security to its bonds (Ex. E to Finding, fol. 80), upon the very same trusts however as are expressed in a certain trust deed heretofore executed by the party of the first part to the party of the second part.

January 8, 1878, the assignees gave notice of this assignment to the Central Co., (Ex. F. to Findings, fol. 81.)

January 4, 1879, the garnishees took possession of the Central Road under their mortgage. At the same time "with the acquiescence of the Central Company but without any assignment of the lease," the garnishees took possession of the Northern Road, and retained possession until May, first 1879 (9th Finding, fol. 43), and up to the time of the service of the process in this action had not paid any one for the use of such road.

After the garnishees took possession of the Northern Road they notified the Northern Company, and Hoyt as trustee under the lease and as assignee thereof, that they had taken possession but would not assume or ratify the lease or be bound by it; neither the Northern Company nor Hoyt paid any attention to this notice nor interfered with the possession of the Northern Road by the garnishees. The garnishees retained possession of the road until May first, and this proceeding was brought to attach the rent for that period.

Upon the first of May, 1879, all parties in interest, including the Central Company, consented to a decree in the foreclosure suit hereinbefore mentioned, by which the lease was abrogated, and a receiver appointed, who leased the Northern Road to the trustees. (Ex. G. fol. 83.)

July 7, 1879, this proceeding was instituted. July 23, 1879, Hoyt as such assignee and trustee, and the garnishees as trustees of the Wisconsin Central Company, with the assent of said company, made a compromise as to the rent by which the garnishees agreed to pay $28,258.44, for the use of the Northern Road during that period from January 4 to May 1st, 1879, and they paid the same over to Hoyt upon receiving a bond of indemnity. (fol. 46 & fol. 88.)

The statutory provisions supposed applicable are as follows :

Section 2753. Either at the time of issuing the summons, or at any time thereafter before final judgment, in any action to recover damages founded upon contract, express or implied, *or upon judgment or decree or at any time after the issuing, in any case, of an execution against property*, and *before the time when it is returnable*, the plaintiff, *or some person in his behalf, may make an affidavit, stating that he verily believes that some person, naming him, is indebted to, or has property, real or personal, in his possession, or under his control belonging to the defendant (or either or any of the defendants) in the action or execution, naming him*, and that such defendant *has not property not liable to execution, sufficient to satisfy the plaintiff's demand*. And that *the indebtedness or property mentioned in such affidavit is to the best of the knowledge and belief of the person making such affidavit, not by law, exempt from seizure or sale upon execution*. Any number of garnishees may be embraced in the same affidavit, *but if a joint liability be claimed against any, it shall be so stated, and the garnishees named as jointly liable, shall be deemed jointly proceeded against ;* otherwise the several garnishees shall be deemed severally proceeded against.

Section 2754. The plaintiff shall annex or subjoin

to such affidavit a garnishee summons, which shall be substantially in the following form :

Court, County,

A. B., *plaintiff*,
vs.
C. D., *defendant*,
E. F., *garnishee*.

The State of Wisconsin :—To the said garnishee : you are hereby summoned, pursuant to the annexed affidavit, as garnishee of the defendant, C. D., and required, within twenty days after the service of this summons upon you, exclusive of the day of service, to answer according to law, whether you are indebted to, or have in your possession or under your control, any property, real or personal, belonging to such defendant, and to serve a copy of your answer on the undersigned at   , in the county of   ; and in case of your failure so to do, you will be liable to further proceedings, according to law. *Of which the said defendant will also take notice.*

L. M., *Plaintiff's Attorney.*
P. O. address,   , County, Wis.

Section 2756. *The garnishee-summons and annexed affidavit shall be served on each of the several garnishees named, in the manner provided in section two thousand six hundred and thirty-six and two thousand six hundred and thirty-seven, for service of a summons in an action; and except where service of the summons in the action is made without the State, or by publication, also on the defendant to the action, in like manner, either before or within ten days after service on the garnishee.* When the defendant shall have appeared in the action by an attorney, such service may be made upon such attorney or upon the defendant. Unless the garnishee-summons be so served on the defendant or his attorney, or the proof of service on the garnishee show that, after due dilligence, such service cannot be made within the State, the service on the garnishee shall become void and of no effect from the beginning.

Section 2754 provides that the garnishee may file and serve an affidavit flatly denying liability, if he does he is discharged, unless the "plaintiff serve notice that he elects to take issue upon the answer to the garnishee-summons, and will maintain him to be liable as garnishee. In which case the issue shall stand for trial as a civil action in which the affidavit on the part of plaintiff shall be deemed the complaint, and the garnishee's affidavit the answer thereto."

Section 2760. *Unless the garnishee shall make the affidavit provided for in the preceding section* (that he does not own or has not property), *he shall, within twenty days from the service of the garnishee-summons, file and serve, in like manner, an affidavit, in which he shall state —*

1. Whether he was, at the time of the service of the garnishee-summons, or has since become indebted, or under any liability to the defendant named in the garnishee-summons, in any manner or upon any account, specifying, if indebted or liable, the amount, the interest thereon, or the manner in which evidence, when payable, whether an absolute or contingent liability, and all the facts and circumstances necessary to a complete understanding of such indebtedness or liability. When the garnishee shall be in doubt respecting any such liability or indebtedness, he may set forth all the facts and circumstances con-

cerning the same, and submit the question to the court.

Section 2765. *The defendant may, in all cases, by answer duly verified,* to be served within twenty days from the service of the garnishee-summons on him, *defend the proceeding against any garnishee,* upon the ground that the indebtedness of the garnishee, or any property held by him, is exempt from execution against such defendant, *or for any other reason is not liable to garnishment; or upon any ground upon which a garnishee might defend the same; and may participate in the trial of any issue between the plaintiff and garnishee for the protection of his interests.* And the garnishee may, at his option, defend the principal action for the defendant, if the latter does not, but shall be under no obligation so to do.

Section 2766. The proceeding against a garnishee shall be deemed an action by the plaintiff against the garnishee and defendant as parties defendant, and all the provisions of law relating to proceedings in civil actions at issue, including examination of the parties, amendments and relief from default or proceedings taken, and appeals, and all provisions for enforcing judgment, shall be applicable thereto; but when the garnishment is not in aid of an execution, no trial shall be had of the garnishee action, until the plaintiff shall have judgment in the principal action, although it may be noticed for trial; and if the defendant have judgment, the garnishee action shall be dismissed with costs. The court shall render such judgment in all cases as shall be just to all the parties, and properly protect their respective interests, and may adjudge the recovery of any indebtedness, the conveyance, transfer, or delivery to the sheriff, or any officer appointed by the judgment, of any real estate or personal property disclosed, or found to be liable to be applied to the plaintiff's demand, or by the judgment pass the title thereto ; and may therein, or by its order, when proper, direct the manner of making sale, and of disposing of the proceeds thereof, or of any money, or other thing paid over or delivered to the clerk or officer. The judgment against a garnishee shall acquit and discharge him from all demands by the defendant, or his representatives, for all money, goods, effects, or credits, paid, delivered, or accounted for, by the garnishee, by force of such judgment.

Section 2767. *When the answer of the garnishee shall disclose that any other person, than the defendant, claims the indebtedness or property in his hands, and the name and residence of such claimant, the Court may, on motion, order that such claimant be interpleaded, as defendant, to the garnishee action ;* and that notice thereof, setting forth the facts, with a copy of such order, in such form as the Court shall direct, be served upon him, and that after such service shall have been made, the garnishee may pay or deliver to the officer or the clerk such indebtedness, or property, and have a receipt thereof, which shall be a complete discharge from all liability to any party for the amount so paid, or property so delivered. Such notice shall be served in the manner required for service of a summons in a civil action, and may be made without the State, or by publication thereof, if the order shall so direct. Upon such service being made, such claimant shall be deemed a defendant to the garnishee action, and within twenty days shall answer, setting forth his claim or any defense the garnishee might have made. In case of default judgment may be rendered, which shall conclude any claim upon the part of such defendant.

The garnishee Stewart was not served, but the garnishee Abbot who was served, undertook to answer for himself and his co-trustee, against whom the plaintiff was seeking, to proceed as upon a joint liability, and to set out all of the facts, and pray the judgment of the Court if they were liable.

Under the provisions of sec. 2767 the garnishees might have disclosed that Hoyt claimed this indebtedness and have given his name and residence so that he could have been made a party.

Or, they might have tendered him the defence of this action. And then the real parties to this dispute could have been before the Court.

The garnishees did not do this. And the Northern Company, as it may under section 2765, is making the defence.

The real parties in interest in the suit are the bond holders of the Milwaukee and Northern company and the defendants in error.

And the real questions to be decided are to whom were the garnishees liable for the use and occupation of the Northern Road from January 4 to May 1, 1879. And whether if the garnishees were liable to the Northern company that liability was attached in this proceeding.

The case was tried by the court, a jury having been waived, which has found the facts as above stated, and upon the facts so found has entered judgment charging the garnishees. There is no dispute as to the facts. No bill of exceptions. If the facts found justify the conclusions of law and the statute has been complied with, the judgment must stand, otherwise it must be reversed.

Assignment of Errors.

First. The Circuit Court erred in holding that a fund had, in some way, accrued, which was to be divided or distributed in this proceeding.

Second. In holding that the garnishees were not liable to the Central company for the use of the Northern road for the period in question.

Third. In holding, as a matter of law upon the facts found, that the garnishees were not liable to Hoyt as trustee under or assignee of the lease, because the holding of the garnishees was in defiance of the lease from the Northern company to the Central company, and in opposition thereto.

Fourth. In holding that the garnishees were liable directly to the Northern company upon the facts found, so as to be charged by these proceedings.

Fifth. In holding that such liability was attached by the proceedings in the record, and in rendering judgment therefor against the garnishees and the Northern company.

I.

The Circuit Court erred in considering that this was a contest as to who should be entitled to a fund which had been created by agreement between the parties or some of them, or in some other manner.

At the time of the service of the process there had been no agreement between any of the parties to this proceeding as to the amount of rent to be paid by the garnishees for the use of the Northern road, except such as the law implies, from the entry and occupation of the road by the garnishees, with the assent of the Central company. The road was at the time of the entry by the garnishees, in the possession of the Central company under its lease from the Northern company. This process was served July 7, 1879, and the only agreement found was made between the garnishees and Hoyt as trustee and assignee of the lease, on the 23d of July, 1879. Whatever claim the plaintiff below had was fixed by the service on the seventh. There was then no fund. The rights of all parties rested in their contracts, as found in the record, and what had been done under them. This may not be very material, because it does not appear that the Central company was a party to the agreement, whatever it was, and the Central company was, under the lease, entitled to the possession of the Northern road, and entitled to the rental thereof from the garnishees after it let them in, so that no agreement as to the amount of rental would be valid unless the Central company was a party to it, but it is the first error, and leavens the whole decision.

As to the Northern road, Stewart and Abbot were strangers. They were not even trustees as to that road. When they took possession of that road they did it either by agreement with the party entitled to the possession, or as trespassers upon the rights of the party entitled to the possession. If by agreement they are liable to the party with whom they agreed upon the terms of that agreement. If they went in and occupied as trespassers, then they were liable, as trespassers, to the party upon whose rights they trespassed.

They were not a court ; they could not summon the parties; lay hold of the road and operate it, and thereby create a fund and distribute it. They had made an agreement with the Central company, merely to the effect that they might enter and operate the Northern, without terms as to rental or length of term. They had made overtures to the Northern company and to Hoyt as assignee and trustee, and both refused to treat with them on the subject ; so that there was no fund by agreement when this process was served. The agreement of July 23d between the garnishees and Hoyt, as assignee and trustee in the mortgage of the Northern company, trustee in and assignee of the lease, did not attempt to create a fund, it merely fixed the amount as between the parties to it, which the garnishees who were liable to somebody for the use and occupation of the road, or for a trespass, should pay to Hoyt as trustee, &c., if he turned out to be the person entitled to demand the rent of the road, or the damages for the entry. If it should turn out that the Central company or some one else was the party entitled to demand the pay, then the agreement was of no account whatsoever. It certainly did not create a fund to be administered.

II.

The Central company was in possession of the Northern road, at the time of the entry by the garnishees under the lease from the Northern company. That lease was valid. The Central company let the garnishees into the occupation of the Northern road

without assigning the lease. That made the garnishees tenants of the Central company, sub-tenants
of the Northern company, liable to the Central company, on *quantum meruit*, for the use and occupation; not liable at-law to the Northern company;
nor to Hoyt as trustee or assignee. Admit that
under *Thomas* vs. *R. R. Co.*, 101 U. S., 71, the
Northern company had no authority to lease its road
when it executed the lease, Ex. B., folio 66. Yet
the Central company went into possession and occupied until they let the garnishees in. Therefore
the rights and remedies flowing out of a valid lease
accrued to each of the parties. *Woodruff* vs. *Erie
Co.*, 93 N. Y., 609.

After the passage of Chapter 292 of the laws of
1874, authorizing railroad companies to lease their
roads, and the supplemental contract of June 1st,
1875 (Ex. C. to finding), confirming the original
lease, it was at least, from that day, a valid lease.
There was no immorality in the contract, nor
anything to avoid it save the lack of power.
When the power was given the confirmatory deed
made the lease valid, and the Central company had
the right of possession of the Northern road for the
remainder of the term. When it let the garnishees in
it had the actual possession as well as the right of
possession. It did not assign the term (9th finding,
fol. 45).

It could let the garnishees in so long as there
was nothing in the lease to prohibit underletting

upon such terms as it could obtain. It could exact a greater rent or could let for less rent, or for shorter term, and the garnishees so let in would be sub-lessees or under-tenants, liable to their lessor, the Central company, for the rent. If the amount of the rent was not fixed by the lease, then it would be what the premises were reasonably worth, but the going in and occupying with the acquiescence of the Central company, create the relation of landlord and tenant between the Central Co., entitled to possession, and the garnishees.

> Taylor's Landlord and Tenant, 636;
> Woodfall L. & Tenant, 2d Ed.; 693;
> Wood's L. & T., Sec. 549, and Note;
> *Holford* vs. *Hatch*, 1 Douy, 183:
> *Cripps* vs. *Blank*, 9 D. & R., 480;
> *Marquis of Camden* vs. *Batterbury*, 50 Q. B.,
> N. S., 808;

III.

And the payment by the garnishees to Hoyt, after the garnishment of such money as the use and occupation of the road was reasonably worth, did not make the garnishees tenants of the Northern company. It merely, *protanto*, discharged the Central company's liability to Hoyt upon the original lease.

The Central company was so badly insolvent that the trustees had seized its road; upon this seizure the Central company let the garnishees into posession of the Northern road upon a tenure by which the garnishees were not liable at law to Hoyt, the trustee in, and assignee of, the lease, nor to the Northern company. Hoyt could by bill alleging the facts against the Central company, and the garnishees who had notice of this insolvency, have collected rent from the garnishees. *Wood's Land & T.* Sec. 554, 1 Story, Eq. 687, Fonbl. B. 1, ch. 3 § 3.

Again, the rent in this case was to be a specified portion of the earnings of the leased property. The language is, "yielding and paying rent therefor, as follows, to wit: In and for each year of the term wherein the gross earnings received from the demised premises, as hereinafter set forth, shall exceed the sum of one million dollars, *thirty per cent. of such gross earnings,* and in and for each year of said term, when the gross earnings shall exceed eight hundred thousand dollars, but not exceed one million dollars, thirty-three per cent.," &c., "upon the first day of February, 1874, the second party (Central company) shall state to the first party (Northern company) an account, as nearly as practical, of the gross earnings received from and upon the demised premises during the month of December, 1873 * * * and upon said first day of February * * * the second party shall pay the amount of rent so approximated * * * to such trustee as shall be from time to time jointly selected," &c. This, I take it, is a reservation of this percentage of the earnings of the property, in specie, as much as would be a reservation of one-third of the crops grown upon a farm, of which reservation the garnishees had knowledge, constructive, if not actual, because taking posession of the Northern road from the Central company, they were charged with inquiry as to the title of the Central company, and with knowledge of whatever that inquiry would develop. When they found that the tenure of the property was such that the trustee in the lease was entitled as rent to a certain proportion of the gross earnings—if they took the whole earnings—they were chargeable with the duty of making over to the trustee the proportion of the earnings to which he was entitled. *Ketchum* vs. *St. Louis*, 101 U. S. 306 ; *Clavoring* vs. *Withery*, 3 P. W., 402.   Unless, as the Court below state in its third conclusion of law, the occupation and operation of said road by Stewart and Abbot, trustees, was not under said lease, but in defiance thereof and in opposition thereto.

Was the occupation and operation of the road by the garnishees not under the lease but in defiance thereof, and in opposition thereto?

The court has found as facts (Fourth finding). That on the 9th of November, 1873, the Northern company leased the Central company its railway, &c., for the term of 999 years from and after November 30, 1873. (Ex. B.) That by supplemental agreements (Ex. C and D), Hoyt was appointed trustee, that the lease was assigned to Hoyt and Greenleaf and notice given. (Ex. E and F.) That the Central company entered into possession of said road under said lease and continued therein until the garnishees, Stewart and Abbot, took possession of said railway in January, 1879, and said company paid rent under said lease ; that such possession was with the acquiescence of the Central company, but without any assignment of the lease.   (9th Finding, fol. 45.)

It is true, they find that Stewart and Abbot notified the Northern company and Hoyt, upon taking possession of the Northern road, that "they declined to assume, affirm or in any way ratify the lease thereof by the Wisconsin Central company, but unless the parties notified should otherwise elect, they would

continue to operate the Northern road temporarily,
and for such compensation as that service might be
fairly worth, and requesting a personal interview to
ascertain their wishes, etc. *But they did remain in
possession*, notwithstanding this notice. There was
no surrender of the lease, nor of possession under it.
What is there in these facts to justify the conclusion
that the entry or subsequent holding was *not* under
the lease or was in defiance thereof and opposition
thereto? How could the Central company let any
one occupy that road who would not be in under
that lease? Who would not have to resort to that
lease to sustain his entry and possession if they were
attacked?

How could the garnishees be in "with the aquies-
ence of the Central company," and be "in in defiance
to the lease and in opposition thereto? If the court
mean simply that the immediate landlord of the garnishee was not the Northern Co., and the immediate
holding was not under that lease, that is, of course,
what we have been trying to demonstrate, but then
what becomes of the clause "in defiance thereof and
in opposition thereto"?

But suppose the entry and occupation were in defiance of the lease and in opposition thereto? They
must have been trespasses. The road belonged to
the Northern company, and it had made the lease
to the Central company; nobody could enter and occupy in defiance of the lease and not be in in the wrong,
not be guilty of a trespass, and that trespass would
be a trespass against the Central company. No one
else had either possession or right of possession. It
would not be a trespass against the Northern company, because the Northern company did not have

the right of possession. The liability of the tres-
passer would not be a liability belonging to the
Northern company, and if it were, it could not be
attached in this proceeding. It would be a liability
in damages, and only debts can be attached under
section 2768.

IV.

The garnishees were not liable to the Northern
company.

There was neither privity of contract nor of estate
upon which the Northern company could found an
action against the garnishees, upon the facts found.

> Taylor, 109, 448;
> Wood's Land. & T., 395;
> 1 Platt on Leases, 9, 101–2;
> *Penly* vs. *Watts*, 7 M. & W., 607;
> *Walker* vs. *Hatton*, 10 M. & W., 249;
> *Bedford* vs. *Terhune*, 30 N. Y., 453;
> *Stilman* vs. *Van Buren*, 100 N. Y., 439;
> *Campbell* vs. *Stetson*, 2 Met., 504;
> *Cross* vs. *Upson*, 17 Wis., 638;
> *Mariner* vs. *Crocker*, 18 Wis., 264.

Of course, if the Central company had omitted to
pay the rent *and the Northern company had paid
it*, it could have maintained an action upon the covenant to pay the trustee for the use of the Northern
company, and have recovered the rental it had paid;
but it could not maintain that action against an un-
der-tenant unless upon bill in chancery charging the
insolvency of the Central company, treating the rent
as due in specie and averring the payment of the
rent by the Northern company.

V.

The garnishees being trustees, are proceeded against jointly. The liability is not attached, except by service upon both, and the service in the record is not sufficient to charge the garnishees.

The proceeding is against the garnishee for a joint liability—only one has been served : Stewart was not found, and Abbot has undertaken to appear and answer for him.

This the garnishee could not do so as to bind his creditor. The proceeding is purely statutory, and the attachment grows out of a compliance with the statute. A garnishee cannot voluntarily appear and substitute his creditor's creditor for his own, *because that goes to the jurisdiction of the subject,* not to jurisdiction of his person.

Steen vs. *Norton,* 45 Wis. 417.
Edlen vs. *Hatsche* 31, N. W. Rep., No. 1. 57.
Laidlaw vs. *Morrow,* 44 Mich. 547.

These garnishees were trustees, not partners ; all are one person in the law. This is a proceeding *in rem* to seize this debt — both trustees are indispensable parties ; *Barney* vs. *Baltimore,* 6 Wall, and cases. Maybe Mr. Stewart would have answered, setting out Hoyt's claim, if he had been served. This debt could not be attached without serving both (Perry on trusts, 411) ; and the fact that the garnishee, Abbot, undertook to help the plaintiff below out by answering that Stewart resided and still is beyond the jurisdiction (fol. 14), does not make the matter any better ; the right to have Stewart served before the difference is charged is the right of the defendant and not of the garnishee.

For these errors the judgment below should be reversed.

E. MARINER,
Attorney for Plaintiff in error.

SUPREME COURT OF THE UNITED STATES.

THE MILWAUKEE & NORTHERN RAILWAY CO.,
Plaintiff in Error,

vs.

THE BROOKS LOCOMOTIVE WORKS.

BRIEF FOR DEFENDANT IN ERROR.

JAMES G. JENKINS,
F. C. WINKLER,
Counsel.

DAVIS, RIESS & SHEPARD,
Attorneys.

KING, FOWLE & KATZ, PRINTERS.

SUPREME COURT OF THE UNITED STATES.

OCTOBER TERM, 1886. No. 226.

THE MILWAUKEE & NORTHERN RAILWAY COMPANY, PLAINTIFF IN ERROR,

vs.

THE BROOKS LOCOMOTIVE WORKS.

On the 6th day of September, 1873, the Brooks Locomotive Works sold and delivered to the Milwaukee & Northern Railway Company a locomotive, which the latter paid for only by its notes. (*Record, p. 23.*)

Two months afterwards, on the 8th day of November, 1873, the same railway company made a lease of its road, with all its power and rolling stock, subject to a mortgage thereon to the Wisconsin Central Railroad Company, for a period of nine hundred and ninety-nine years, "provided the agreements, covenants, and stipulations made therein by the party of the second part were faithfully performed; and until breach, if any, thereof by the second party, its successors or assigns." (*Record, p. 24; Exhibit B, p. 38.*)

Among the covenants of the party of the second part, are covenants to operate the road in connection with and as part of its own road. The rent reserved is a percentage of the "gross earnings" of the demised road, the rate being from 30 to 35 per cent., dependent upon the amount of gross earnings. "Gross earnings" are defined in the lease itself as *gross receipts*, less all taxes. By the terms of this lease the rent reserved was payable to a trustee, who was to apply them primarily in payment of the interest on the bonded debt (secured by mortgage) of the demised road. Under this lease all the property of the Milwaukee & Northern road, including, of course, the locomotive mentioned, passed into the possession of the Wisconsin Central Railroad Company. (*Record, p. 24.*) By a subsequent agreement between the two railroad companies a larger percentage "of the gross earnings received from the demised premises" was agreed to be paid, and to be accepted by the Milwaukee & Northern Railway Company, "in lieu of the rent reserved in the lease," etc. (*Exhibit C, Record, p. 42.*) Jesse Hoyt was afterwards designated as the trustee, to whom the rent, under the lease, should be paid. (*Exhibit D, Record, p. 45.*) By an instrument dated January 7, 1878, the Milwaukee & Northern Railway Company, "in order further to secure the payment of its first mortgage bonds," assigned to Jesse Hoyt and A. Warren Greenleaf, the trustees for its bondholders, the lease dated November 8, 1873, "and all and singular the covenants of the Wisconsin Central Railroad Company in said lease contained, and each and every modification thereof, and all moneys due or to grow due thereon." (*Record, p. 24; Exhibit E, p. 47.*) In 1875 suit was commenced against the Milwaukee & Northern Railway Company in the Circuit Court of the United States for the Eastern District of Wisconsin, to foreclose the mortgage securing the bonds of that company. (*Record, p. 24.*) On the 28th day of April, 1879, James C. Spencer was, in said suit, "appointed receiver of all and singular the property, estate and effects of the said Milwaukee & Northern Railway Company particularly described in the trust deed set forth in the bill of complaint." (*Exhibit G, Record, p. 48.*) The receiver qualified May 5, 1879. (*Record, p. 24.*) The roads of said two railroad companies were connecting lines.

The Wisconsin Central Railroad Company had, on the 1st of July, 1871, mortgaged its lines and appurtenances to Edwin H. Abbot and John A. Stewart, as trustees, to secure its bonds; the mortgage giving power to the trustees, upon default, to take possession. (*Record, p. 23.*)

On the 4th day of January, 1879, Messrs. Abbot and Stewart, as such trustees, default having been made, took possession of the Wisconsin Central Railroad, and also took possession of the Milwaukee & Northern Railway, and thereupon notified the Milwaukee & Northern Railway Company and Jesse Hoyt of the taking of such possession, but that they would not assume any obligation under the lease to the Wisconsin Central Railroad Company, that they declined to assume, affirm, or in any way ratify that lease, and that unless said parties should otherwise elect, they would continue to operate said Milwaukee & Northern Railway temporarily for such compensation as that service would be fairly worth. (*Record, pp. 8, 25; Exhibit E, p. 19, and Exhibit H, p. 49.*) Neither the Milwaukee & Northern Railway Company or Jesse Hoyt made any objection, and Abbot and Stewart operated the Northern road without further arrangement, until James C. Spencer was appointed receiver as aforesaid, when they entered into a lease with him for a term commencing May 1, 1879. (*Record, pp. 9, 25-6.*)

In the meantime the Brooks Locomotive Works had recovered judgment in the U. S. Circuit Court for the Eastern District of Wisconsin against the Milwauke & Northern Railway Company for the price of the unpaid locomotive, and on the 7th day of July, 1879, garnished Edwin H. Abbot and John A. Stewart, trustees, as debtors of the Milwaukee & Northern Railway Company, in accordance with the laws of the State of Wisconsin. The Wisconsin Central Railroad Company and Charles L. Colby were also made parties to the suit of garnishment. (*Record, pp. 23, 1 and 2.*)

The Wisconsin Central Railroad Company and Charles L. Colby answered, simply denying all liability to the Milwaukee & Northern Company. (*Record, pp. 5 and 6.*)

The Milwaukee & Northern Railway Company, the judgment debtor, claiming this right under Section 2765 of the Revised Statutes of Wisconsin, answered as follows:

"And now comes said Milwaukee and Northern Railway Company, defendant, by E. Mariner, its attorney, and in answer to said garnishment shows that the said Wisconsin Central Railroad Company, Charles L. Colby,

Edwin H. Abbot, and John A. Stewart and Edwin H. Abbot, as trustees, were not nor was any or either of them indebted to said M. & N. R'y Co. at the time of the service of said garnishee process, and had not, nor had any or either of them in his or its possession, nor under his or its control any property, estate or effects whatsoever of the Milwaukee & Northern Railway Company liable to such garnishment; that said Stewart and Abbot, as trustees as aforesaid, were in possession of the railroad of said Milwaukee & Northern Railway and operating the same under and by virtue of a lease theretofore made between said Edwin H. Abbot and John A. Stewart, as trustees, and James C. Spencer, as receiver of the Milwaukee & Northern Railway, appointed by said court in a certain cause therein pending in equity, in which Jesse Hoyt, trustee, was complainant, and this defendant, the Milwaukee & Northern Railway Company, the Wisconsin Central Railroad Company and others were defendants, by the terms of which lease the rent was payable to said Spencer as such receiver; wherefore this defendant prays judgment that such proceedings may be dismissed with costs." (*Record, p. 4.*)

Edwin H. Abbot answers in behalf of himself and John A. Stewart, trustees. (*Record, p. 7, 8 and 9.*)

After stating that himself and Stewart are trustees of the Wisconsin Central R. R. under a deed of trust and mortgage dated July 1, 1871. and as such were garnished as debtors of the Milwaukee & Northern Railway Company on behalf of the Brooks Locomotive Works on the 7th of July, 1879, the lease of November 8, 1879, and supplemental agreements, and notice of assignment of said lease, and the taking possession of the Wisconsin Central Railroad by the trustees, he proceeds:

"That when they took possession, as aforesaid, they found said Wisconsin Central Railroad Company was operating the Milwaukee & Northern Railway under the lease and agreements aforesaid; that said trustees refused to recognize and accept said lease in any manner or form, and refused to ratify the same or to operate said

Milwaukee & Northern Railway under the same, and never did recognize, accept or ratify said lease or operate said railway under it, but declined absolutely to assume any obligation whatever under that lease, and so notified the Milwaukee & Northern Railway Company and said Jesse Hoyt, as he was the president of said railway company, and the surviving trustee under its first mortgage and bonds, and the trustee under the lease of the Milwaukee & Northern Railway Company to the Wisconsin Central Railroad Company, and the assignee of said lease named in said notice of said alleged assignment thereof, and served upon said Hoyt a certain notice in writing, copy of which is hereto annexed and marked Exhibit E, and also served upon one Angus Smith, as he was the vice-president of said Milwaukee & Northern Railway Company, and the agent in Milwaukee of said Jesse Hoyt, a copy of said notice on the same day, to wit, the 11th day of January, A. D. 1879.

Sixth. That said trustees Stewart and Abbot remained in possession, as aforesaid, of the Milwaukee & Northern Railway until the 1st day of May, A. D. 1879, without objection from any of the parties interested in said railway, and during the intervening period received the earnings thereof; that subsequently, on the 23d day of July, A. D. 1879, upon an accounting together, it was agreed by and between said Stewart and Abbot, as trustees as aforesaid, and said Jesse Hoyt, as president of the Milwaukee & Northern Railway Company, and as trustee of the Milwaukee & Northern Railway Company, and surviving trustee under its first mortgage and bonds, and trustee under its lease of its railway to the Wisconsin Central Railroad Company, and assignee of said lease under alleged assignment thereof from said Milwaukee & Northern Railway Company, and in any and every other capacity wherein said Hoyt represented said railway, said Hoyt being then and there the president of said Milwaukee & Northern Railway Company, that the sum of twenty-eight thousand, two hundred fifty-eight and forty-four one-hundredths dollars ($28,258.44) was the amount and the only amount payable by said trustees Stewart and Abbot to the party lawfully entitled to receive the same out of the moneys received by said trustees Stewart and Abbot from the operation of the Milwaukee & Northern Railway since the 3d day of January, A. D. 1879, to the 1st day of May, A. D. 1879, in full settlement of all account thereof between said trustees and the parties interested in said railway and in full settlement for said trustees, Stewart and Abbot, operation of said railway during said period; that said sum of twenty-eight thousand, two hundred fifty-eight and forty-four one-hundredth dollars ($28,258.44) was the reasonable and fair rental, and the whole amount properly to be paid by said trustees for the use and occupation of the railroad of the Milwaukee & Northern Railway Company while so in possession of the said trustees Stewart and Abbot; that this sum was in possession of said trustees Stewart and Abbot in their capacity of trustees, as aforesaid, at the date of the service aforesaid upon them of the garnishee summons in the above entitled action; and the said Stewart and Abbot, being in doubt as to whether the facts and circumstances aforesaid, which are fully and truthfully set forth, cast any liability as garnishees upon them, have answered fully and hereby submit the question of their liability to the court.

(Signed)   EDWIN H. ABBOT,
                                  Trustee as Aforesaid.

Formal issue was taken, and the case tried by the court in May, 1883, a jury being waived. The finding states the facts of which the substance has been heretofore given, and as stated in the answer of Abbot and Stewart. It also finds as facts that the lease of November 8, 1873, was not assigned by the Wisconsin Central Railroad Company to Abbot and Stewart, and that they did not, between the 3d of January and 1st of May, 1879, hold the Northern road under lease from Spencer, receiver, and that compensation for its use and occupation by them during that period was not owing to the receiver. (*Record, pp. 25, 26.*)

It also contains the following finding: "*Tenth.* That on the 8th day of March, 1880, an order was made in the foreclosure suit of the mortgage of the Milwaukee & Northern Railway Company for the sale of said railroad, which sale took place on the 5th of June, 1880, and was sold to Ephraim Mariner and Guido Pfister, as trustees for the holders of the bonds under said mortgage; that on the 9th day of June the report of sale was filed and was confirmed by the court, and that thereafter, on the 3d day of July, 1880, the final report of the receiver was filed, asking for a discharge, and said report was confirmed on the 5th day of July, 1880." (*Record, p. 26.*)

The court held that the compensation for use and occupation of its road during the period in question by Abbot and Stewart was owing to the Milwaukee & Northern Railway Company, and hence gave judgment against the garnishees.

To review this judgment two writs of error have been sued out, one in favor of the Milwaukee & Northern Railway Company and one in the name of Abbot and Stewart.

There is no bill of exceptions. The only question therefore, presented by the record is, whether the judgment against Abbot and Stewart is justified by the pleadings and findings.

In affirmation of this, we invite the Court to the following CONSIDERATIONS:

I.

There is a writ of error by the Milwaukee & Northern Railway Company.

This corporation has no interest in the judgment; neither has nor claims to have any right affected by it. Its contention is that the money adjudged to be paid over to the plaintiff is not *its* money. It is not, and it cannot in the nature of things, be aggrieved by the judgment. Why, then, should this company have its writ of error?

It will be claimed that although it has no interest,

it has the right to defend under the following provision of the Wisconsin Revised Statutes :

§ 2765.   The defendant may, in all cases, by answer, duly verified, to be served within twenty days from the service of the garnishee summons on him, defend the proceedings against any garnishee, upon the ground that the indebtedness of the garnishee, or any property held by him, is exempt from execution against the defendant, or for any other reason is not liable to garnishment ; or upon any ground upon which the garnishee might defend the same ; and may participate in the trial of any issue between the plaintiff and garnishee for the protection of his interests."

We submit that the only rational interpretation this statute can receive is that the defendant may contest the garnishee proceeding upon any ground so far as his own interests are concerned.   This is reasonable.   But to allow the defendant to wage a contest, where the garnishee admits a liability, and the defendant in no way makes a claim to the fund on which the admission rests, is so absurdly antagonistic to all accepted notions of legal controversy, that the legislature cannot be supposed to have intended it.

In section 3 of chapter 161 of the laws of 1871, of Wisconsin, it was provided, that "the defendant may appear in such garnishee proceeding, at the time such garnishee is required to answer, and file *   * a notice in writing, stating that he claims the property, money, credits, effects or indebtedness * * as exempt from seizure or sale on attachment or execution, or any other facts tending to show that the person or corporation so summoned is not liable to be garnisheed, which notice shall state fully the facts upon which he claims that such property, money, etc., are exempt, or that such person or corporation is not liable to be garnisheed, and such defendant may also be sworn * * and be examined in relation to facts stated in such notice, and shall be and become a party to said garnishee proceedings."

The revisers in reporting their revision, say of section 2765:

"This section takes the place of section 3, chapter 161, 1871, and is designed to afford the defendant the right to fully protect his interests, not only as against the plaintiff, but also when the garnishee denies liability against him." (Reviser's Notes, p. 200.)

Thus the history and avowed purpose of the enactment of § 2765 show that it was intended for no other purpose than to afford the defendant complete protection when his interests are imperiled by the garnishment.

We submit, therefore, that the writ of error of the Milwaukee & Northern Railway Company should be dismissed.

II.

But the writ of the garnishees, Abbot and Stewart, remains. The answer of these garnishees is put in under the last provision of Subd. 1, Sec. 2760 Revised Statutes of Wisconsin, which provides: "When the garnishee shall be in doubt respecting any such liability or indebtedness, he may set forth all the facts and circumstances concerning the same, and submit the question to the Court."

Section 2767 provides that, "When the answer of the garnishee shall disclose that any other person than the defendant claims the indebtedness or property in his hands, and the name and residence of such claimant," the latter shall be made a party to the proceeding and set up his claim.

Neither the answer of the garnishees nor that of the defendant, the Milwaukee & Northern Railway Company, discloses any *claimant* in this case. If they had, the claimant would have been brought in to assert his title and specify on what it is founded. We would have a definite issue. And if he *disclaimed* that would end the controversy in his behalf.

As it is, the defense contents itself with the general contention that some one other than the defendant is the *owner*, though not the claimant, of the admitted indebtedness. It is necessary, therefore, to examine the various grounds of possible ownership.

1. It is alleged in the answer of the Milwaukee & Northern Railway Company that Abbot and Stewart occupied the road by virtue of a lease from James C. Spencer, receiver. This is an evident mistake. The sum in question is due from Abbot and Stewart for occupation of the road from January 3d till May 1st, 1879.

The receiver was not appointed till April 28th, and did not qualify till May 5th, 1879. He then took possession of the road and leased it to Abbot and Stewart for a term commencing May 1st, and from that time forth received the rents. With the fund in question which had accrued before his appointment the receiver had nothing to do.

It may have been within the power of the Court to take possession of this fund through its receiver, but it did not do so.

The appointment of the receiver was made in persuance of negotiations between the parties and the order was entered by consent (See *ninth* finding, *Record p.* 25). The evident purpose of the order was the making of a lease to Abbot and Stewart. This was done, and beyond this and the collection of the rents under that lease, the receiver never made any claim or demand, or had or pretended to have any possession.

Hence, this garnishment cannot be dismissed on the ground of any rights in the receiver.

    American Bridge Co., vs. Heidelbach, 94 U. S. 798.
    Noyes, Receiver, vs. Rich, 52 Me. 115.
    Gilman vs. Ill. & Miss. Tel. Co., 91 U. S. 603.
    Galveston R. R. Co. vs. Cowdry, 11 Wall 459.

"A receiver *pendente lite* is a person appointed to take charge of the fund or property to which the receivership extends, while the case remains undecided. The *title* to the property is not changed by the appointment."

    Keeney vs. Home Ins. Co., 71 N. Y. 401.
    Beaston vs. Farmers' Bank, 12 Peters 102.
    High on Receivers, § 5.

It is to be observed, too, that *the answer of Abbot and Stewart, the garnishees,* in the statement upon which

they submit the question of their liability to the Court—
and upon which it would seem *their* writ of error must
be decided—does not make any mention of the appointment of a receiver, or any claim in his behalf.

If any doubt, however, remains as to a right of the
receiver, *the conclusive answer is found in the fact* that before the trial of this cause the road was sold under
decree in the foreclosure suit and "that thereafter on
the 3d of July 1880, *the final report of the receiver* was
filed, asking for a *discharge,* and said report was confirmed on the 5th day of July, 1880." (See *tenth* finding,
Record p. 261.)

This *establishes* that he was never made receiver of
this fund. The suit in which he was appointed was at
an end before this case was tried.

2. Jesse Hoyt is not entitled to this rent as surviving trustee under the mortgage. It has been explicitly
ruled that such trustees are entitled to the revenues of
the road only after taking possession or at least making
a regular demand for them.

    Galveston R. R. vs. Cowdrey, 11 Wall. 459.
    Gilman vs. Ill. & Miss. Tel. Co., 91 U. S., 603.
    Am. Bridge Co. vs Heidelbach, 94 U. S. 798.

It is expressly found, as indeed is manifest, "that
said trustees (the trustees under the mortgage) had never
taken possession of said railroad and property under said
mortgage nor claimed so to do, until the appointment
of said receiver." (See *sixth* finding, *Record p.* 24.)

3. A further question is, Did Mr. Hoyt acquire any
right to these moneys by virtue of the assignment by the
Northern railway company to him of the lease to the
Wisconsin Central Railroad, or as trustee named in said
lease ?

This manifestly could only be so, if it was money
payable by virtue of that lease.

Messrs. Abbot and Stewart did not take possession
under or by virtue of the lease to the Wisconsin Central
road. They expressly repudiated it, and promptly notified all parties that they would not hold under the lease,
but would operate the road temporarily at a fair compen-

sation. They invited negotiations for a new arrangement.

Who could make a new arrangement with them ? Who could let to them ? Who but the owner of the reversion, the Northern road ? Certainly not Jesse Hoyt as assignee of the lease or as trustee for the receipt and disbursement of the rents, named in the lease.

The assignment of the lease by the lessee gave to the assignee the right to receive the rent reserved, and nothing more. It amounted simply to a transfer of the tenant's covenant to pay rent; the property itself, the reversion, remained in the lessee. He alone, not the assignee of the rent, could re-enter if the conditions of the lease were broken, or take possession if the lessee abandoned it.

> *Huershel vs. Lorillard*, 6 Robertson, 260.
> *Willard vs. Tillman*, 2 Hill, 274.
> *Watson vs. Hunkins*, 13 Iowa, 547.
> *Hunt vs. Thompson*, 2 Allen, 341.
> *Perrin vs. Lepper*, 34 Mich., 292.
> *Dixon vs. Nicholls*, 39 Ill., 372.
> *Leonard vs. Burgess*, 16 Wis., 41.

It will scarcely be contended that what has been called an assignment of the lease in this case, the instrument marked Exhibit "E" (*See Record p. 47*) is anything more than an assignment of the rents reserved by lease, or gave to the assignees the slightest interest in the property or reversion. Hence if the money in question is not owing as rent upon this lease, the assignees can as such have no claim to it.

We have already shown that Messrs. Abbot and Stewart did not enter under that lease, that they refused to hold under it, that they so advised parties interested, at the same time stating that they would, for the time being, operate the road, paying a fair remuneration. It remains to be said that this was during the short period here in question acquiesced in by all parties in any way concerned. (See *ninth* finding, *Record p. 25*). It is idle therefore to say that the remuneration due which accrued by reason of this occupation was rent reserved by the lease.

There was no assignment of the lease by the Central company to Abbot and Stewart or of any interest in it, or right under it. It has been ruled in Wisconsin that while a party other than the lessee found in possession of demised premises is presumed to hold as assignee of the lease, the presumption may be rebutted by proof that he never in fact had such assignment.

Cross vs. Upson, 17 Wis. 618
Mariner vs. Crocker, 18 Wis. 251.

Here, it is expressly found that the garnishees operated the road "without any assignment of the lease." (Record, p. 25.)

4. The chief contention of our opponents in the Court below remains to be examined, viz: That title to the moneys in question vested in the Wisconsin Central Railway Company so as to defeat their garnishment as a credit of the Northern road. The sum and substance of the argument is this: The Central road was the lessee for 999 years. Its lease had not expired. Abbot and Stewart going into possession with the acquiescence (as it is claimed) of the Central road, became *its* tenants, and hence owe *it* for the use and occupation.

The unsoundness of the position lies in the circumstance that it overlooks certain material facts.

First of all let us examine the nature of this lease. It is true that its nominal term was 999 years, i. e. it was 999 years "provided the agreements, covenants, and stipulations made herein by the second party are faithfully performed, and *until breach*, if any, thereof by the second party, its successors or assigns." [*Habendum, Rec. p.* 38.]

An all-important covenant on the part of the Central road is "to operate the same (the Northern road) in connection with and as part of its own road." (*Sixth paragraph, Rec. p. 40.*) This is not only a covenant, but it is one without the continued performance of which the lease can scarcely be conceived to exist. The rent reserved consists not of fixed sums to be paid out of the treasury of the lessee, but is a *pro rata* division between the lessee and the lessor of the revenues *received* from the operation of the road. When the lessee ceases to operate, it ceases to *receive*, it has no receipts to divide, the rent must cease.

Now the Wisconsin Central company not only broke its covenant to operate this road, but it became impossible for it to keep it. It could operate it at all only in connection with its own road. But it was evicted from its own road under a superior power antedating its undertaking to operate the Northern in connection therewith. What could it do? The trustees refused to take or operate under the lease. That is not only admitted but strongly asserted in their answer. Evicted from its own, what could the Wisconsin Central company do but abandon the operation and possession of the Northern road? This is the sum and substance of what was done. The only possession possible under the lease was the operation of the road. Absolutely incapacitated for such possession, its complete abandonment was not a choice but a necessity. The garnishees took possession not under the lease but in spite of it, not under the Central company as its tenants, but in total disregard of any rights or claims that company might make. It made none. It *acquiesced*. This acquiescence, found by the court as a fact, is laid hold of by our learned opponents as strong aid to their position to establish Abbot and Stewart as under-tenants of the Central road. But the acquiescence was in *the manner* of the possession as well as the fact of possession. The guarnishees, to use the language of their answer, "refused to recognize and accept said lease in any manner or form, and refused to ratify the same or to operate said railway under the same." In this the Central road acquiesced. The garnishees did not enter as tenants of the lessee. If they had it would have been a simple matter to arrange such terms as they wanted. If the Central company had claimed still to have the possession under its lease, it could have sublet (if at all) at any rent, however trifling, which might be agreed upon. But such was not the action of the parties. The Central company, unable to perform the lease, abandons it. The garnishees take possession, not under this

company making terms with it, but in manifest nega-
tion of any rights on its part, address themselves directly to the landlord, the Northern road, offering to
operate it for the present at what it may fairly be worth.
The Central road acquiesces. The landlord makes no objection, enters into negotiation resulting in a new lease
after May 1st, and agrees to the *quantum meruit* for the
interval. Jesse Hoyt may have had many capacities, but
he was also president of the Northern road. Prior to
the appointment of the receiver the Northern road was
the landlord. It was the only being that could grant a
lease. It held the property. Upon abandonment of its
lease by the Central road the possession necessarily re-
verted to it. Abbot and Stewart refused to hold under
the Central—proposed to deal with the owner direct.
This was accepted and acquiesced in by all parties concerned. No one dreamed of such a thing as the Central
still in possession and Abbot and Stewart as its tenants.
Not an act was done consistent with this theory. The
possession of the Central was ended. It was treated by
everybody as at an end. The garnishees did not address
themselves to the Central company, asking it for terms
on which they might hold as its tenants. They recog-
nized that the occupation by this company was gone,
that it would pay no rent under the lease for the future,
and so they make offer to the landlord to temporarily occupy and pay what it is worth. They in effect promise to
pay the *owner*, whoever that may be. That was the Northern road, and the rent thus accruing must be its property,
unless it had been prior to our garnishment in some manner transferred. That we have shown had not been done.

It was with the representatives of the Northern
Railway company that the garnishees adjusted the
amount to be paid for their temporary occupation. The
Central company was not consulted about it. (See answer of garnishees. *Record, p. 9.*) It is true this was after
the garnishment, but it reflects the understanding of the
parties concerned to the effect that the possession of the
garnishees was under the owner and not under the Central Company.

In entire consistency with this theory, the Central company makes no claim to this money. It is a party to the proceeding. It sets up no claim, and in its answer denies that it is in any way indebted to the Northern road, which would not be true if the lease had continued in force after it abandoned possession.

What right, then, have these garnishees or any one in their name, to insist that in spite of its not claiming it, the Central must have this fund?

It has been argued that if the money is adjudged to belong to that company, Jesse Hoyt will, under, one or another of his trusteeships, have an equitable claim to it. It is needless to follow the dialectics by which this is sought to be established. The record discloses no equity in Jesse Hoyt, whatever.

III.

It has been argued that the bondholders have an equitable claim upon this money. Undoubtedly the bondholders, as well as the defendant in error, had equities against the Northern road. They gave their money, we our locomotive, towards its construction and equipment. They have had nearly all the earnings since November, 1873, they have the whole road, and have had our engine almost from the day it was delivered—we have had nothing. Now, if a receiver of the road had been appointed at the suit of the bondholders at the time the lease to the Wisconsin Central was made (less than three months after sale and delivery of the locomotive to the railroad company then in possession) the Court in the exercise of its equitable jurisdiction, would have directed him to pay for this engine out of the earnings of the road.

Fosdick vs. Schall, 99 U. S., 235.
Miltenberger vs. Logansport, 106 U. S., 286.
Union Trust Co. vs. Souther, 107 U. S., 591.
Burnham vs. Bowen, 111 U. S., 776.
Turner vs. I., B. & W. R'y Co., 8 Bissell, 315.

The lease put the whole income into the hands of

the bondholders. The whole rent was paid to them. The purchase of necessary power and rolling stock for a railroad is a "current expense," creates "a debt of the income" within the meaning of the above cases. "What may properly be termed the debts of the income," says Chief Justice Waite in *Burnham vs. Bowen*, supra, "should be paid from the income before it is applied in any way to the use of the mortgagees," and, again, "if current earnings are used for the benefit of mortgage creditors before current expenses are paid, the mortgage security is chargeable in equity with the restoration of the fund which has been improperly applied for their use."

It is very clear, therefore, that in equity this money ought to go to pay the debt in question.

IV.

The record not only shows that the defendant in error has a superior equity, but it fails to show that the bondholders have any claim at all.

It is found 'that the road has been sold and bought in for the bondholders, the sale confirmed, and that the receiver has settled his accounts and been discharged. (See *tenth* finding, *Record, p. 26.*) With the exception of the little sum here in dispute, these bondholders therefore have all the assets of this road, the road itself, and all that it has earned since November, 1873. It does not appear that this does not pay them in full. It does not appear that a single dollar of principal or interest due to them remains unpaid.

Ought not that fact to be decisive of this case? What decent excuse can those who are waging this defense, not for their own protection, but for the avowed benefit of other parties, give, except that although under a foreign flag, they are in fact enlisted in the cause of the bondholders?

This Court can guess at no equities which the record does not disclose, and it is certain that it does not show one unpaid bondholder.

The Northern Railway Company itself has passed out of existence. It does not appear that with the exception of the demand of the present claimant a single unpaid debt survives it. None of the parties to the record (except the defendant in error) claim for themselves any right to the money in question. On whose behalf then, can this court be asked to reverse the judgment under review ?

JAMES G. JENKINS,
F. C. WINKLER,
Counsel for Defendant in Error.

DAVIS, RIESS & SHEPARD,
Attorneys.

APPENDIX.

We append so much of the Wisconsin Revised Statutes relating to garnishment as is in any way material.

Section 2755 provides what the plaintiff's affidavit shall contain.

Section 2756 gives the form of summons.

Sections 2755 and 6 provide the mode of service.

Section 2757 authorizes additional garnishments and changes of venue.

Section 2758 requires filing of papers.

Section 2759 gives form of answer by affidavit where all liability is denied.

"Section 2760. Unless the garnishee shall make the affidavit provided for in the preceding section he shall within twenty days from the service of the garnishee summons, file and serve in like manner, an affidavit in which he shall state:

1. Whether he was, at the time of the service of the garnishee summons, or has since become indebted, or under any liability to the defendant named in the garnishee summons, in any manner or upon any account, specifying, if indebted or liable, the amount, the interest thereon, the manner in which evidenced, when payable, whether an absolute or contingent liability, and all the facts and circumstances necessary to a complete understanding of such indebtedness or liability. When the garnishee shall be in doubt respecting any such liability or indebtedness, he may set forth all the facts and circumstances concerning the same, and submit the question to the court.

2. Whether he held at the time aforesaid, or now holds, the title or possession of any real estate, or any interest in land of any description, or of any personal property, effects or credits, or any instruments or papers relating to any such, belonging to the defendant, or in which he is in any wise interested. And if he shall admit any such, or be in doubt respecting the same, he shall set forth a description of such property, and all

the facts and circumstances concerning the same, and the title, interest, or claim of the defendant, in or to the same.

3. If he shall claim any setoff, or defense, to any indebtedness or liability, or any lien or claim to such property, he shall set forth the facts and circumstances thereof fully.

4. He may state any claim of exemption from execution, on the part of the defendant, or other objection known to him, against the right of the plaintiff to apply upon his demand, the indebtedness or property disclosed.

5. If he shall disclose any indebtedness, or the possession of any property to which the defendant, and any other person as well, make claim, he may set forth the names and residences of such other claimants, and, so far as known, the nature of their claims."

Section 2761 provides for proceeding in case of failure to answer..

Section 2762 authorizes garnishee to pay over admitted indebtedness.

Section 2763 provides mode of taking issue on answer.

Section 2764 authorizes answer by officer of a corporation or by an agent of a garnishee.

"Section 2765. The defendant may, in all cases, by answer, duly verified, to be served within twenty days from the service of the garnishee summons on him, defend the proceeding against any garnishee, upon the ground that the indebtedness of the garnishee, or any property held by him, is exempt from execution against such defendant, or for any other reason is not liable to garnishment; or upon any ground upon which a garnishee might defend the same; and may participate in the trial of any issue between the plaintiff and garnishee for the protection of his interests. And the garnishee may, at his option, defend the principal action for the defendant, if the latter does not, but shall be under no obligation so to do."

"Section 2766. The proceeding against a garnishee shall be deemed an action by the plaintiff against the garnishee and defendant as parties defendant, and all the provisions of law relating to proceedings in civil actions at issue, including examination of the parties, amendments and relief from default or proceedings taken, and appeals and all provisions for enforcing judgments shall be applicable thereto; but when the garnishment is not in aid of an execution, no trial shall be had of the garnishee action until the plaintiff shall have judgment in the principal action, although it may be noticed for trial; and if the defendant have judgment, the garnishee action shall be dismissed with costs. The court shall render such judgment in all cases as shall be just to all the parties, and properly protect their respective interests, and may adjudge the recovery of any indebtedness, the conveyance, transfer or delivery to the sheriff, or any officer appointed by the judgment, of any real estate or personal property disclosed, or found to be liable to be applied to the plaintiff's demand; or by the judgment pass the title thereto; and may therein, or by its order, when proper, direct the manner of making sale and of disposing of the proceeds thereof, or of any money or other thing paid over or delivered to the clerk or officer. The judgment against a garnishee shall acquit and discharge him from all demands by the defendant, or his representatives, for all money, goods, effects or credits paid, delivered or accounted for by the garnishee, by force of such judgment."

Section 2767. When the answer of the garnishee shall disclose that any other person than the defendant claims the indebtedness or property in his hands, and the name and residence of such claimant, the Court may, on motion, order that such claimant be interpleaded as a defendant to the garnishee action; and that notice thereof, setting forth the facts, with a copy of such order, in such form as the Court shall direct, be served upon him, and that after such service shall have been made, the garnishee may pay or deliver to the officer or the clerk such indebtedness or property, and have a receipt therefor, which shall be a complete discharge from all liability to any party for the amount so paid, or property so delivered. Such notice shall be served in the manner required for the service of a summons in a civil action, and may be made without the State, or by publication thereof, if the order shall so direct. Upon such service being made, such claimant shall be deemed a defendant to the garnishee action, and, within twenty days, shall answer, setting forth his claim, or any defense which the garnishee might have made. In case of default, judgment may be rendered, which shall conclude any claim upon the part of such defendant.

Section 2768. From the time of the service of the summons upon the garnishee, he shall stand liable to the plaintiff to the amount of the property, moneys, credits and effects in his possession, or under his control, belonging to the defendant, or in which he shall be interested, to the extent of his right or interest therein, and of all debts, due or to become due, to the defendant, except such as may be, by law, exempt from execution. Any property, moneys, credits and effects held by a conveyance or title, void as to the creditors of the defendant, shall be embraced in such liaiblity.

Supreme Court of the United States.

OCTOBER TERM, 1886.

No. 226.

BROOKS' LOCOMOTIVE WORKS

vs.

THE MILWAUKEE AND NORTHERN RAILWAY COMPANY.

F. C. WINKLER,
Of Counsel for Defendant in Error.

JUDD & DETWEILER, PRINTERS.

BROOKS' LOCOMOTIVE WORKS

vs.

THE MILWAUKEE AND NORTHERN RAILWAY COMPANY.

Under point V. of the brief of plaintiff in error it is objected that the garnishee *Stewart* was not served with process, and that therefore the judgment cannot be maintained. This point is here raised for the first time.

It is claimed, however, that no judgment is maintainable without such service and that it is a fatal error, though not mooted below.

We answer:

I.

We proceed against Abbott and Stewart for a joint liability. Abbott was served, and he was answerable for the whole sum which he and Stewart held jointly. The fund in question accrued in Wisconsin, was in Wisconsin, and was bound by the service on Abbott in Wisconsin.

Drake on Attachment, § 475.

If there is error it is only in this, that there is a personal judgment against Stewart as well as against Abbott.

II.

Who is in position to complain of error in this matter?

It is said the garnishee cannot voluntarily appear, cannot waive service, because it is the *debtor's* not his own property that is involved (Steen *vs.* Norton, 45 Wis., 417); therefore the *defendant* can allege the error, although the garnishee may have attempted to waive it.

But, as we have already seen, the defendant *here* disclaims any interest in the fund in question. How, then, can *it* complain even if the garnishees should choose *to confess* judgment in our favor.

But if the garnishee can waive no defect in the service because the proceeding is against defendant's property and not his own, *that defendant* certainly, when *he* appears, under section 2765, Revised Statutes, to defend the proceeding, must see to the proper service of process first—before he answers to and tries the merits.

The garnishee summons is accompanied by an affidavit, which constitutes the complaint. When the defendant has come in and answered that affidavit, and had a trial upon that issue, it is certainly too late for him to say that there was no garnishee process which he was bound to answer at all.

We have a writ of attachment in our State which, before

being executed, is required to have a certain affidavit annexed. It is provided that the defendant may traverse the affidavit, and on the issue thus raised a trial is had by the court. Will any one claim that a defendant may traverse and try the truth of that affidavit, and, when beaten at that, claim that the writ was not properly served?

It is the same with the garnishee process. By appearing and answering to its merits the party against whose property it is directed inevitably admits due service.

The Northern Railway Company here has appeared in the garnishee proceeding and answered. (Record, p. 4.) It has defended Abbott and Stewart on their liability as garnishees by traverse of the affidavit of garnishment, and a trial has been had on the merits. It is too late for that defendant to complain of a defect of service.

When the defendant has thus waived any objections he might make, and the garnishees have also fully submitted themselves to the court, answered to the merits, appeared at the trial, as these garnishees have done (Rec., pp. 7, 21), it is too late for them, too, to claim that the service was defective.

A garnishee cannot waive any rights of the defendant, but, of course, he may waive his own.

Hoyt *vs.* Robinson, 10 Gray, 371.
Sabine *vs.* Cooper, 15 Gray, 532.

III.

But there was no defect of service. Stewart was a nonresident and could not be served in the State of Wisconsin. The service of part of several joint debtors, as garnishees, where those not served are non-residents of the State, is binding on all. If it were not so, garnishment as a remedial agent would be weak indeed.

> Drake on Attachment, §§ 477, 562, 563, 565.
> Parker *vs.* Danforth, 16 Mass., 299.
> Warner *vs.* Perkins, 8 Cush., 518.
> Atkins *vs.* Prescott, 10 N. H., 120.
> Peck *vs.* Barnum, 24 Verm., 75.
> Anderson *vs.* Wanzer, 5 How. (Miss.), 587.

That these garnishees were trustees can make no difference. As to us they were no trustees, but simply joint operators for a time of the Northern road. They bore no trust relation to that road. Their liability arises simply from the fact of their occupation.

F. C. WINKLER,
Of Counsel for Deft. in Error.

Lightning Source UK Ltd.
Milton Keynes UK
UKHW05f0705100918
328632UK00007B/650/P